Book-Talk

Book-talk

Exciting Literature Experiences for Kids

Michelle O'Brien-Palmer

illustrations by
Denny Driver

MicNik Publications

Credits

Illustrations and Cover: Denny Driver
Educational Consultant: Lori Blevins Gonwick
Cover Photography: Lance O. Kenyon
Copy Editor: Laura Utterback
Content Editors:
Suzie Fiebig, Teacher, Kirkland, WA
Suzie Fiebig's 2nd-grade students
Eileen Gibbons, Teacher, Rochester, NY
Lori Blevins Gonwick, Teacher, Kirkland, WA
Lori Blevins Gonwick's 3rd-grade students
Martha Ivy's 4th-grade students
Marci Larsen, Principal, North Bend, WA
Valerie Marshall's 4th-grade students
Ruby Pannoni, Communication Arts Resource Specialist, Harleysville, PA
Sue Parker, Teacher, Redmond, WA
Sue Parker's 6th-grade students
Mary Schneider, Teacher, Woodinville, WA
Dr. Katherine Schlick Noe, Professor, Seattle University, Seattle, WA
Joyce Standing's 5th-grade students
Japhy Whalen's 4th-grade and 5th-grade students

Young Authors:

Lissa Rubin, Kindergartener
Lechelle Lucas, 1st-grader
Terry Yoo, 2nd-grader
Steven Yoo, 2nd-grader
Nick Palmer, 3rd-grader
Erin Rubin, 3rd-grader

Brian Schnierer, 3rd-grader
Philip Sanchez, 4th-grader
Shannon Bovan, 4th-grader
Brandon Schnierer, 5th-grader
Juleah Swanson, 5th-grader
Kaili Ka'lua'hini'nui Jackson, 6th-grader

ISBN 1-879235-02-1
Library of Congress Catalog Card Number: 93-91418
Copyright © 1993 Michelle O'Brien-Palmer

Manufactured in the United States of America
10 9 8 7 6 5 4 3 2 1

ATTENTION: SCHOOLS AND BUSINESSES

Books from MicNik Publications are available at quantity discounts with bulk purchase for educational, business, or sales promotional use. For information, please write to:
MicNik Publications
P.O. Box 3041, Kirkland, WA 98083
(206) 881-6476

Acknowledgements

I would like to thank the following people for their support and contributions in the creation of *Book-Talk*.

I am especially grateful to the children who kid-tested, edited and provided project recommendations, quotes and inspiration for *Book-Talk*. You have all been instrumental in the creation of this book.

- Thanks to Suzie Fiebig's second-graders for kid-testing forms and for your wonderful story map, Venn Diagram and puppet examples. I thoroughly enjoyed your smiles, hugs and help.
- Thanks to Lori Blevins Gonwick's third-graders for kid-testing forms, great group feedback, story map example, and lively literature groups. I enjoyed every minute in your classroom.
- Thanks to Valerie Marshall and Martha Ivy's fourth-graders for sharing your weekly literature circles. Your groups were pivotal in the creation of Chapter Five.
- Thanks to Japhy Whalen's fourth- and fifth-graders for your straightforward editorial support. Many changes were made as a result of your comments.
- Thanks to Joyce Standing's fifth-graders. Your excitement toward literature and learning is captivating. Your insightful comments and enthusiastic support were wonderful.
- A special thanks to Sue Parker's sixth-graders for your weekly editing sessions. Your attention to detail and the responsible way in which you carried out your role as editors was very impressive. Your editorial comments and suggestions significantly impacted *Book-Talk*. Also, the time and effort you spent conducting your "books recommended by kids" survey will help other readers to find their special book. Thanks to Molly Brown for your rainbow idea.

I also extend sincere thanks to those who helped in the production of this book:

To the young authors for their examples of how to fill out the various forms and their actual projects – Lissa Rubin, Lechelle Lucas, Terry Yoo, Steven Yoo, Nick Palmer, Erin Rubin, Brian Schnierer, Philip Sanchez, Shannon Bovan, Brandon Schnierer, Juleah Swanson and Kaili Ka'lua'hini'nui Jackson.

To the editors for their dedication and enriching contributions to this book – Suzie Fiebig, Eileen Gibbons, Lori Blevins Gonwick, Marci Larsen, Ruby Pannoni, Sue Parker, Dr. Katherine Schlick Noe, and Mary Schneider.

To Lori Blevins Gonwick for her support and great ideas as the educational consultant, to Denny Driver for his delightful illustrations, to Laura Utterback for her professional editing support and great genre ideas, to Gail Schroder for her fine detail work, and to Lance O. Kenyon for his cover photograph.

Also, thank you Gid and Nick. I appreciate your encouragement and support. I love you both very much.

Dedication

Book-Talk is dedicated to every child involved in this book.

Suzie Fiebig's 2nd-Grade Class

Samantha Arnold	Alyna Holden
Jessica Berg	Elizabeth Hughes
Miriam Brambila	Paul Jones
Amber Cass	Hallie Luginsland
Ryan Clark	Madelyne Martinka
Derek Cruse	Oleg Mastikash
Erin Dooley	David Moneymaker
Tim Denning	Chris Otte
Jessica Dressen	Aaron Schmalle
Hassan Eisa	Danny Spurr
Jesse Fox	Jake Standley
Christopher Freni	Derek Voelker
Aaron Gwaltney	Elissa Wildenborg
Milad Ghazvini	Peter Zanassi

Lori Blevins Gonwick's 3rd-Grade Class

Marisa Brambila	Leah Moore
Andrew Burns	Jeremiah Nusbaum
Emily Dean	Brandon Ohm
Steven Demlow	Brett Ortiz
Brien Dodd	Christian Polocoser
Alice Fairbairn	Robby Ricker
Matt Fillmore	Seth Robins
Justin Ford	Lindsey Rose
Justin Frei	Taylor Shalan
Ford Harris	Renee Stokes
Cynthia Hsu	Lynnsey Sturgeon
Michelle Kay	Miychell Vereeke
Karla La Hoz	Isaiah Washington
Eugene Litvin	Matthew Wood

Japhy Whalen's 4/5th-Grade Class

Rubin Beyerlin	Clayton Martin
Jessica Blanch	Wade Miller
Shannon Bovan	Carolin Puloka
My-Lan Dodd	Michael Ragen
Kasi Farrar	Jonathon Robinson
Rachelle Ford	Delano Rogers
Taris Graham	Lo Chon Saeturn
Kelsey Holt	Geoff Teeter
Dawn Hoskins	Lela Tyson
Cameron Lomax	Victor Victorino
Sean Leverentz	Alerenzo Webb
Fala Mathly	

Joyce Standing's 5th-Grade Class

Zach Carver	Emily Mack
Jackie Ciliberti	Matt McMurrer
Mike Corby	Brianna Risch
Stephen DeShazo	Andy Schneider
Mollie Durkin	Katherine Spiers
Andy Fawcett	Kirsten Thomas
P.J. Gordon	Tony Volpe
Mitch Kearns	Alexis Waite
Blake Laabs	Kristin Ware

Young Authors

Shannon Bovan
Kaili Jackson
Lechelle Lucas
Nick Palmer
Erin Rubin
Lissa Rubin
Philip Sanchez
Brandon Schnierer
Brian Schnierer
Juleah Swanson
Steven Yoo
Terry Yoo

Valerie Marshall's and Martha Ivy's 4th-Grade Class

Tina Acena	Timothy Hood	Chris Shearer
Devin Austria	Lauren Humphrey	Megan Stauffer
Eric Anderson	Christopher Huson	Kenny Steele
Matthew Black	Brandon Jaffe	Mark Stracione
Adam Borchardt	Eric Karm	Michelle Theriault
Colleen Carbrey	Brian Kim	Shana Thirtyacre
Lynn Chealander	Brian Macinnes	Cari Thomas
Heather Cochrane	Bradley Marsee	Brynda Vela
Mark Crockett	Jonathan Marshman	Jack Vu
Kristin Culleton	Jason Mattax	Jessica Walker
Brian Dailey	Jessica Michelman	Matthew Warren
Katharine Dunn	Ashley Milligan	Tori White
Thomas Fowler	Brett Norville	
Ryan Frankland	Daniel Paris	
Todd Hannant	Brandon Poyfair	
Chris Hartsell	Tara Rooney	
Laura Hernandez	Stuart Rowe	
Timothy Hood	Natalia Sanoja	
Lauren Humphrey	Marissa Sawyer	

Sue Parker's 6th-Grade Class

Scott Blake	Rei Kayabashi
Jillian Bloxham	Andy Kim
Dale Chhen	Gil Mazurek
Molly Clark	Hanna Molmberg
Britni Curtis	Karen Seligman
John Denney	Sheetal Shah
Kentaro Gates	Christian Sindayer
Lisa Heppner	Eli Steurich
Josh Hightree	Nate Weirbach
Leslie Jensen	

Quotes by Others

Tiffany Driver
Ed Lobdell
Tara O'Brien
Gavin Schroder

Table of Contents

LITERATURE GROUPS
Getting Started: Chapter 5

FUN READING PROJECTS: Chapter 6

FUN READING PROJECTS: Continued

REFERENCE BOOKS: Chapter 7

FORMS TO COPY: Chapter 8

Introduction
for parents and teachers

BOOK-TALK: Exciting Literature Experiences for Kids is written to help children (K-6th grade) become lifelong readers, forever *hooked-on-books*.

In this pursuit, *Book-Talk* emphasizes respect for the reader's choice of book and his or her unique response to literature. It is intended to promote thoughtful analysis of what has been read and to validate a reader's experience through open-ended, thought-provoking questions. As sharing is an enriching experience for all involved, *Book-Talk* is written to encourage the reader to share his/her insights into literature through various individual reading projects as well as in nurturing, relaxed literature circles or groups. But most of all, *Book-Talk* is about the joy and exhilaration that comes from reading and sharing one's literature experience.

Although the text speaks to the young reader directly, it will require adult supervision and guidance in most cases. Many chapters include a page defining the main topic and a page giving information about their contents. Whenever more information might be helpful to parents or teachers it will be found in italics just under the top border of a text page. The second chapter (I Love to Read) includes a list of books recommended by kids. It does not reflect the author's reading recommendations or grade level appropriateness. It reflects the children's uncensored list of the books they love to read. If you are interested in a book list recommended by adults, there are many lists available at your local library. There is also a chapter of forms for you to use with your readers at home or school. Make as many copies of these forms as you need. The resource chapter at the end of the book is intended to provide a list of excellent reference books for bringing literature into the home or classroom. I highly recommend these books.

Each idea in this book is meant to be taken as liberally as possible. There is no one right way to do anything. The more variations created, the more exciting the process will be.

Guide, listen and experience each young reader's unique response to literature!

Foreword
Note to Kids

"When I read I feel warm and it has my full attention. I am in the book like I'm my favorite character."

Steven DeShazo,
5th grade

"When I read books I learn about people like George Washington and Abraham Lincoln, and go on adventures in my mind."

Tara O'Brien,
2nd grade

I love to read. When I read a book I can experience different worlds just like the kids in the quotes. A great book takes me on incredible adventures. I enjoy imagining the characters and setting as the author's words paint pictures in my mind.

As I've travelled to many different classrooms and talked with kids about books, I've found that kids love books too. The kids in these classrooms were having so much fun reading that I decided to write a book to share their favorite reading experiences with you. I have included some of their favorite books in *Book-Talk*. See if there are some you've read and others you might be interested in reading. You will also find their recommendations for a variety of fun reading projects and creative ways to share your reading experience with others.

I wish you many wonderful reading adventures!

Chapter 1

Introduction

Introduction to Book-Talk: Exciting Literature Experiences for Kids

This chapter provides a brief introduction to each main chapter. For more detailed information please see the actual chapter. BOOK-TALK was written with the help of over 150 kids. They were part of the writing and editing process. The young authors who share their unedited examples of various forms and reading projects in the book are listed below:

Lissa Rubin	Kindergarten student
Lechelle Lucas	1st- grade student
Steven Yoo	2nd-grade student
Terry Yoo	2nd-grade student
Nick Palmer	3rd- grade student
Erin Rubin	3rd- grade student
Brian Schnierer	3rd- grade student
Shannon Bovan	4th- grade student
Philip Sanchez	4th- grade student
Brandon Schnierer	5th- grade student
Juleah Swanson	5th- grade student
Kaili Jackson	6th- grade student

Illustrations:

The illustrations in this book were selected for their thought-provoking abilities. As in reading, each person will experience the illustrations in their own unique way. The children involved in the creation of *Book-Talk* had fun discussing what they saw in each illustration.

Chapter 2: I Love to Read

This chapter is intended to help readers determine their reading interests, including topic and genre, and help them select their own special book. They are encouraged to list the books they may wish to read in the future and record books as they read them. Readers will find fun ways to write to favorite authors and illustrators, and share this information with their friends.

Chapter 3: Read and Respond

Each person experiences a book in a unique way. This chapter suggests a number of ways readers can respond to literature. There are examples of a response journal, story predictions, story maps, retelling stories and comparing and contrasting literature. Readers are encouraged to share their literature experience with others.

Chapter 4: Read and Review

As we experience the book we are reading, we also evaluate its meaning to us. If it is interesting we keep reading. If it isn't, we lose interest. Read and Review is a chapter which explores fun, exciting ways to review a book. Ideas range from Book-Sells to Pizza Reviews. They are all highly recommended by kids.

Chapter 5: Literature Groups (Getting Started)

A natural way of sharing books is to form literature groups. Younger readers seem to enjoy very small groups of five members or less. Even in the 6th-grade, seven seems to be an ideal number of group members. This chapter is dedicated to helping you form literature groups in your classroom or home. Therefore, a number of group focus ideas have been presented.

Chapter 6: Fun Reading Projects

The excitement of reading a good book is wonderful. This chapter provides projects recommended by kids. These projects are fun and help readers synthesize and apply what they have learned from the books they have read. Each project is kid-tested and approved. Readers will find a project checklist and supply form to to help organize their projects.

Have fun reading!

Chapter 2
I Love to Read

I Love to Read

"I love to read because you become more involved with the story. You feel more for the characters than you would watching the story on TV." Jackie Ciliberti, 5th grade

Reading can take us into unknown worlds: past the barriers, boundaries and limitations of our bodies and life experience. A book can tug at our emotions: making us laugh, cry, scream or shout. It can extend our perceptions of this world and stimulate our imaginations as we enter fantastic new worlds never dreamed of before. When we select <u>our</u> own books and follow <u>our</u> interests, reading becomes a lifelong passion.

This is an especially fun chapter. It helps you determine your interests, select a book, write to your favorite authors and illustrators, and keep track of your reading. This is a time to think about what you like to read and whose books you like to read. Share your ideas with your friends. ***A book is a wonderful gift to share.***

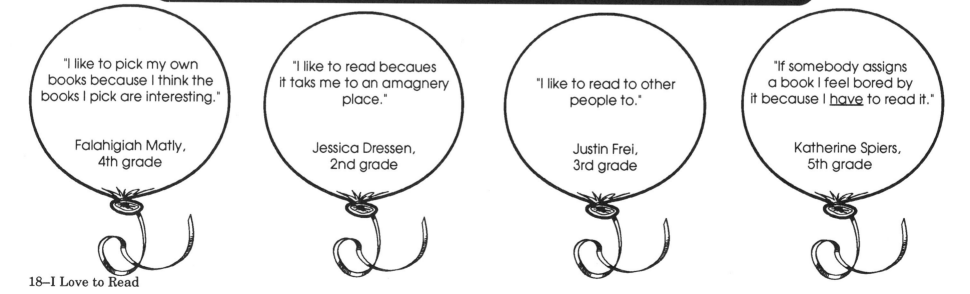

"I like to pick my own books because I think the books I pick are interesting."

Falahigiah Matly,
4th grade

"I like to read becaues it taks me to an amagnery place."

Jessica Dressen,
2nd grade

"I like to read to other people to."

Justin Frei,
3rd grade

"If somebody assigns a book I feel bored by it because I <u>have</u> to read it."

Katherine Spiers,
5th grade

About This Chapter

This chapter includes...

Book Selection

Readers select a book in many different ways.

Book Sharing

Readers can share their favorite authors and illustrators with others.

Genre Trees
Different Types of Books

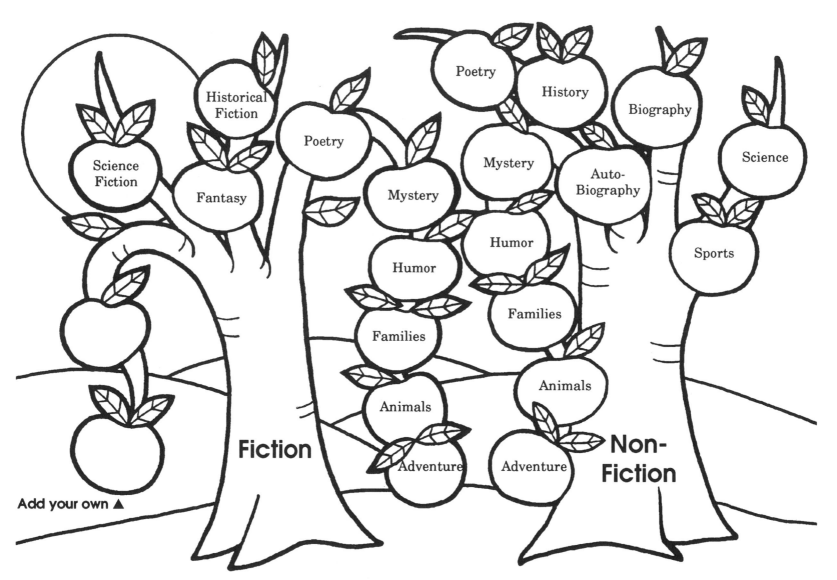

Fiction: Imaginary stories   Non-Fiction: True stories and information

Add your own ▲

Genre Tree Descriptions

Fiction

Adventure
- Exciting imaginary journeys to interesting places
- Spies

Historical Fiction
- Stories of imaginary people based upon historical events
- Made-up stories based upon real people

Mystery
- A crime
- A question to be answered
- An investigation
- Suspense and climax

Realistic Fiction
- Stories based on things that could really happen but didn't
- Stories about imaginary families
- Stories that help us learn about ourselves

Science Fiction
- Stories about possible future events
- Space travel to other galaxies
- Stories about possible future inventions

Fairytales Fantasy
- Dragons, wizards, imaginary characters
- Magic, Once upon a time, heroes, villains
- Good vs. bad, imaginary places

Animals
- Talking animals
- Animals acting like people
- Imaginary stories about kids and their pets

Non-Fiction

Adventure
- Exciting real journeys to interesting places
- Real explorers' journeys
- Real-life heroes

Historical Stories
- Stories about real life in other times
- True stories about real people from the past

Mystery
- A true crime
- True puzzles with no answers
- Unsolved mysteries about creatures like Bigfoot

Families
- Real-life families
- Stories of people and families from all cultures

Science
- Scientific discoveries and inventions
- How things work
- Information about our bodies
- Information about the world and space

Biography
- True stories about real people
- Factual information about famous people

Nature
- The environment
- Taking care of the Earth
- Plant books
- Wildlife books

Interest Sheet

The interest sheet helps younger children think about things they like to do. An adult can then help translate their interests into possible reading topics.

Materials:
Form (copy – page 134)
Pencil/pen

Goals:
To determine your interests
To help select book topics which might
 interest you

Steps:
1. Fill out each of the boxes.
2. Ask an adult to help you write book ideas.
3. Use this list to help you find your next
   book.

Just for Fun:
Think of other things you like (sports,
 picture books, poetry, etc.)

Interest Sheet Example

1. Things I like to do at home

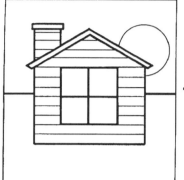

Color
Watch Movies
Play Barbies
Play Piano

Play Freeze tag
Play in my play house

2. Things I like to do at school

Play at recess
I like choosing time
Play with friends
Computer time

3. My favorite movies and t.v. shows

Flintstones

Hook, Aladdin
Beauty and the Beast
Wizard of Oz

4. Things I wonder about

Why do we grow bigger?
How do cars work?
How do we get our voice?
How did we come alive?

Name: Lissa

Book Ideas

1. Animal books
   Musical books
   Picture books
2. Books about school
   " computers
   Family / friends
3. Fairy Tales
   Fantasy books
   Cartoon books
4. Basic-① How bodies work
   ② How cars work

Our Favorite Books List

The students in Sue Parker's 6th–grade classroom, at Ben Rush Elementary School in Redmond, WA, conducted a schoolwide survey to create a list of each student's favorite book. The 6th–graders determined the genre categories and each student placed their book into the category in which they felt it fit. Therefore, this list (book and category) reflects each participating child's choice and perspective.

Materials:
List on pages 25–31

Goal:
To select books using a book list recommended by other kids

Steps:
1. Find the genre (category) of book you like, such as picture books, sports, etc.
2. Find books that look interesting to you.
3. Write these on your "Books I Really Want to Read" form (page 135)

Just for Fun:
Do your own survey in your home, classroom, or school

Books Recommended by Kids

(Students at Benjamin Rush Elementary School, Redmond, WA)

Adventure

Title	Author	Grade
The Littles	John Peterson	Second
Charlie and the Chocolate Factory	Roald Dahl	Third
James and the Giant Peach	Roald Dahl	
Farmer Boy	Laura Ingalls Wilder	Fourth
Watership Down	Richard Adams	
Where the Red Fern Grows	Wilson Rawls	
Hatchet	Gary Paulsen	Fifth
Island of the Blue Dolphins	Scott O'Dell	
Kara, The Lonely Falcon	Joseph Girzone	
The Call of the Wild	Jack London	
Where the Red Fern Grows	Wilson Rawls	
White Fang	Jack London	
Canyons	Gary Paulsen	Sixth
Cigars of the Pharaoh	Herge	
Hatchet	Gary Paulsen	
Homecoming	Cynthia Voigt	
Maniac Magee	Jerry Spinelli	
Mountain of Mirrors	Rose Estes	
On the Far Side of the Mountain	Jean Craighead George	
The Cay	Theodore Taylor	
The Time of the Witch	Mary Downing Hahn	
Tintin in Tibet	Herge	

Fiction

Title	Author	Grade
Henry and Mudge in the Sparkle Days	Cynthia Rylant	Second
Mister Popper's Penguins	Richard Atwater	
Oh, the Places You'll Go!	Dr. Seuss	
The Frog Prince, Continued	Jon Scieszka	
The Grouchy Ladybug	Eric Carle	
Tikki Tikki Tembo	Arlene Mosel	
Charlotte's Web	E.B. White	Third
Different Dragons	Jean Little	
Fourth Grade Rats	Jerry Spinelli	
Fudge-a-mania	Judy Blume	
Full House Same to You Duck	Bonnie Worth	
One Fat Summer	Robert Lipsyte	
Sarah, Plain and Tall	Patricia MacLachlan	
Socks	Beverly Cleary	
The Lion, the Witch and the Wardrobe	C.S. Lewis	
The Addams Family: A Novelization	Stephanie Calmenson	Fourth
The Legend of Huma	Richard A. Knaak	
The Wish Giver: Three Tales of the Coven Tree	Bill Brittain	
Mossflower	Brian Jacques	Fifth
Nothing's Fair in Fifth Grade	Barthe DeClements	
Sideways Stories from Wayside School	Louis Sacher	
The Sign of the Beaver	Elizabeth George Speare	
Where the Red Fern Grows	Wilson Rawls	
Dragonfire Volume 3	Morgana Rhys	Sixth
Prince Caspian	C.S. Lewis	
Winnie-the-Pooh	A.A. Milne	

Humor

Title	Author	Grade
Phil the Ventriloquist	Robert Kraus	Second
Esio Trot	Roald Dahl	Third
Matilda	Roald Dahl	
Beetles, Lightly Toasted	Phyllis Reynolds Nayler	Fourth
Esio Trot	Roald Dahl	
Full House Same to You Duck	Bonnie Worth	
Mrs. Piggle-Wiggle's Magic	Betty MacDonald	
Nothing's Fair in Fifth Grade	Barthe DeClements	
The Fourth Grade Wizards	Barthe DeClements	
There's a Boy in the Girls' Bathroom	Louis Sacher	
BFG	Roald Dahl	Fifth
Hank the Cowdog	John R. Erickson	
Matilda	Roald Dahl	
There's a Boy in the Girls' Bathroom	Louis Sacher	
Alice in Rapture, Sort Of	Phyllis Reynolds Naylor	Sixth
Merry Christmas, Amelia Bedelia	Peggy Parish	
Santa Cows	Cooper Edens	
Sideways Stories from Wayside School	Louis Sacher	
Sixth Grade Secrets	Louis Sacher	

Mystery

Title	Author	Grade
Werewolves Don't Go to Summer Camp	Debbie Dadey / Marcia Jones	Second
Hardy Boys	Franklin Dixon	Third
Lights Out (Fear Street Series)	R. L. Stine	Fourth

Mystery

Title	Author	Grade
Egypt Game	Zilpha Keatly Snyder	Fourth
Great Christmas Kidnapping Caper	Jean Van Leeuwen	
Mystery of the 99 Steps	Carolyn Keene	
Nate the Great	Marjorie Sharmat	
River Heights #1: Love Times Three	Carolyn Keene	
The Boxcar Children #20	Gertrude Chandler Warner	
The Chessmen of Doom	John Bellairs	
The Dead Man in Indian Creek	Mary Downing Hahn	
The Letter, the Witch, and the Ring	John Bellairs	
Bones on Black Spruce Mountain	David Budbill	Fifth
Bury Me Deep	Christopher Pike	
Mystery of the 99 Steps	Carolyn Keene	
Spellbound	Christopher Pike	
Stay Out of the Basement	R. L. Stine	
The Doll in the Garden	Mary Downing Hahn	
The True Confessions of Charlotte Doyle	Avi	
To Grandmother's House We Go	Willo Davis Roberts	
Beach House	R. L. Stine	Sixth
Dead on Target (Hardy Boys Casefiles #1)	Franklin Dixon	
Elizabeth Gail and the Mystery at the Johnson Farm	Hilda Stahl	
Ski Weekend: Fear Street Series	R.L. Stine	
Something Upstairs	Avi	
The Baby-sitter	R.L. Stine	
The Knife: Fear Street Series	R.L. Stine	
The Mystery of the Fire Dragon	Carolyn Keene	
The Overnight: Fear Street Series	R.L. Stine	
The Westing Game	Ellen Raskin	
What Could Go Wrong	Willow Davis Roberts	
Vampire Vacation	Thomas McKean	

Non-Fiction

Title	Author	Grade
Animal Families	Marilyn Mangus	Second
Fire Fighters	Robert Maas	
Kings of Creation	Don Lessem	
Nine True Dolphin Stories	Margaret Davidson	
Rain Forest Secrets	Arthur Dorros	
Reptile	Colin McCarthy, Nick Arnold	
How Long, Great Pumpkin, How Long	Charles M. Schulz	Third
Mysteries of Outer Space	Franklyn Branley	
Abraham Lincoln: The Great Emancipator	Augusta Stevenson	Fourth
Helen Keller	Margaret Davidson	
Lincoln: A Photobiography	Russell Freedman	Fifth

Picture Books

Title	Author	Grade
Arthur's Halloween	Marc Brown	First
Arthur's Nose	Marc Brown	
Arthur's Thanksgiving	Marc Brown	
Berenstain Bears Blaze a Trail	Stan and Janice Berenstain	
Go, Dog, Go!	P.D. Eastman	
Mama, Do You Love Me?	Barabara M. Joosse	
One Fish, Two Fish, Red Fish, Blue Fish	Dr. Seuss	
Owl Moon	Jane Yolen	
Starring First Grade	Miriam Cohen	
Tacky the Penguin	Helen Lester	
Ten in the Bed	Penny Dale	
Ten, Nine, Eight	Molly Bang	
The Cat in the Hat	Dr. Seuss	
The Day the Teacher Went Bananas	James Howe	
The Napping House	Audrey Wood	
Twelve Napping Princesses	Freya Littledale	

Picture Books

Title	Author	Grade
A Porcupine Named Fluffy	Helen Lester	Second
Bailey Goes Camping	Kevin Henkes	
Carl's Christmas	Alexandra Day	
Danny and the Dinosaur	Syd Hoff	
Fox in Socks	Dr. Seuss	
George's Marvelous Medicine	Roald Dahl	
I Just Forgot	Mercer Mayer	
If You Give a Mouse a Cookie	Laura Joffe Numeroff	
Imogene's Antlers	David Small	
Julius, the Baby of the World	Kevin Henkes	
Kites Sail High	Ruth Heller	
Little Grunt and the Big Egg	Tomie de Paola	
Mouse Soup	Arnold Lobel	
On Christmas Eve	Peter Collington	
Pecos Bill: A Tall Tale	Steven Kellogg	
Pinkerton, Behave!	Steven Kellogg	
Prince William	Gloria Rand	
Sylvester and the Magic Pebble	William Steig	
The Talking Eggs	Robert D. San Souci	
The Tale of the Mandarin Ducks	Katherine Paterson	
The Ballad of Mr. Tubbs	Pierre Houde	
The Cake that Mack Ate	Rose Robart	
Tigress	Helen Cowcher	
Willy the Wimp	Anthony Browne	

Poetry

Title	Author	Grade
A Light in the Attic	Shel Silverstein	Second
The Giving Tree	Shel Silverstein	
The New Kid on the Block	Jack Prelutsky	
Where the Sidewalk Ends	Shel Silverstein	

Realistic Fiction

Title	Author	Grade
Changes for Samantha: A Winter Story	Valerie Tripp	Second
Samantha Books	Valerie Tripp	
The Magic School Bus on the Ocean Floor	Joanna Cole	
Socks	Beverly Cleary	Third
Anne of Green Gables	L.M. Montgomery	Fourth
On the Banks of Plum Creek	Laura Ingalls Wilder	
Five Finger Discount	Barthe DeClements	Fifth
Gone with the Wind	Margaret Mitchell	
Little House on the Prairie	Laura Ingalls Wilder	
My Side of the Mountain	Jean Craighead George	
Naya Nuki: Girl Who Ran	Kenneth Thomasma	
Up Periscope	Robb White	
A Little Princess	Frances Hodgson Burnett	Sixth
Alice in Rapture, Sort of	Phyllis Reynolds Naylor	
Avalanche!	An Rutgers Van der Loeff	
Forever	Judy Blume	
Island of the Blue Dolphins	Scott O'Dell	
Little Women	Louisa May Alcott	
Maniac Magee	Jerry Spinelli	

Sports

Title	Author	Grade
Long Shot for Paul	Matt Christopher	Fourth
Tough to Tackle	Matt Christopher	
Magic/Earvin "Magic" Johnson and Richard Levin	Earvin Johnson and Rich Levin	Sixth

Reading Idea List

The idea list helps readers select their next book from a list of books they really want to read. This list can be added to as they learn about new books from book-talks (page 76) or book-sells (page 74).

Materials:
Form (copy – page 135), book list (page 25–31)
Pencil/pen

Goals:
To determine titles for future reading
To continue listing new book ideas

Steps:
1. List the books you want to read.
2. Keep your list handy so you can write new book ideas as you think of them.
3. Check off the book title and record the date when you've finished reading your book.

Just for Fun:
Write down book ideas as you listen to book-talks or book-sells by others at school

Reading Idea List Example

Name: Kaili

Books I Really Want To Read !

Title	Author	Genre	I read it! ✓
Marial of Redwall	Brian Jacques	Fiction	
The Cay	Theodore Taylor	Adventure	✓ 12-10-92
Call of the Wild	Jack London	Adventure	
Sign of the Beaver	Elizabeth George Spear	Fiction	✓ 1-15-93
Sixth Grade Secrets	Louis Sacher	Humor	

Reading Record

This log can be kept separately or in a folder with the Response Journal (page 55).

Materials:
Form (copy – page 136)
Pencil/pen/markers

Goal:
To record the pages you read at each sitting

Steps:
1. Write today's date.
2. Write the name of the book you are reading.
3. Write the page number where you stopped reading.
4. Draw a symbol you design under "page" on the form when you have finished reading your book.

Just for Fun:
Place a special sticker under "page" when you have finished your book
Create your own reading record folder
Keep a reading record at home and school

Reading Record Example

Name: Philip

My Reading Record

Date	My Book Title	Page
1-11-93	Henry and Ribsy	39
1-13-93	"	45
1-15-93	"	53

Genre Sampling

This is a fun way to sample the many types of books available to readers. Readers enjoy brainstorming other genre toppings for the pizza like poetry. Thanks to Lori Blevins Gonwick, 3rd-grade teacher, for her genre sampling ideas.

Materials:
Form (copy – page 137)
Pencil
Large Paper Pizza Shape

Goal:
To read many types of books (genres)

Steps:
1. Choose the genre you want to try first.
2. Find a book in this genre and read it.
3. When you've finished reading your book, write the title and author in the topping.
4. When you have read each of the types of books, celebrate with a pizza.

Just for Fun:
Create your own personal pan pizza

Genre Sampling Example

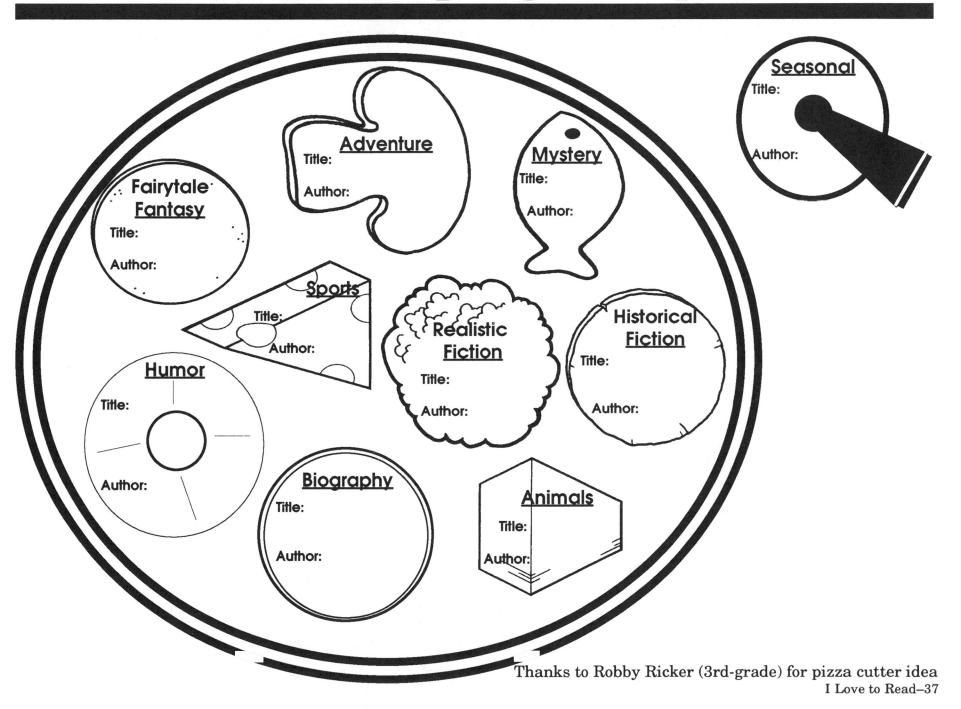

Seasonal
Title:
Author:

Adventure
Title:
Author:

Mystery
Title:
Author:

Fairytale Fantasy
Title:
Author:

Sports
Title:
Author:

Realistic Fiction
Title:
Author:

Historical Fiction
Title:
Author:

Humor
Title:
Author:

Biography
Title:
Author:

Animals
Title:
Author:

Thanks to Robby Ricker (3rd-grade) for pizza cutter idea

Favorite Authors Sheet

A literature group or circle (Chapter 5) is a great place to have readers share their favorite authors with others.

Materials:
Form (copy – page 138)
Pencil/pen/markers

Goal:
To list your favorite authors and the books they've written

Steps:
1. After reading a book you especially liked, write the author's name in the center of one cloud.
2. Write the book titles outside the cloud.
3. Share your favorite authors list with your friends.

Just for Fun:
Look in the library for other books by these authors and write them on your reading list
Examine the writing style of a favorite author and try writing in a similar style

Favorite Authors Example

Name: Erin

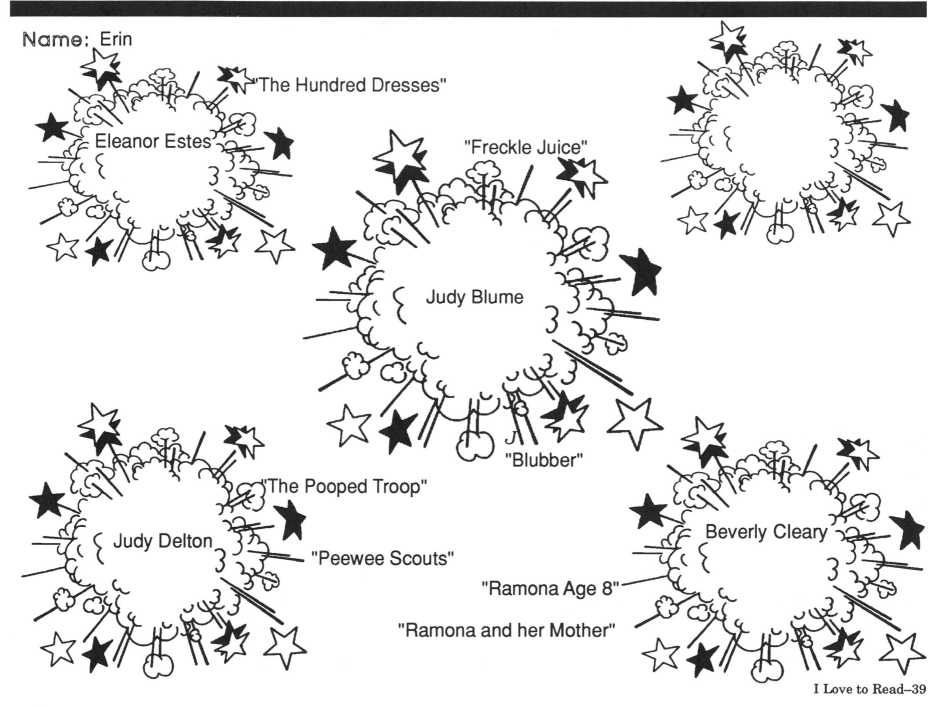

"The Hundred Dresses"

Eleanor Estes

"Freckle Juice"

Judy Blume

"Blubber"

Judy Delton

"The Pooped Troop"

"Peewee Scouts"

Beverly Cleary

"Ramona Age 8"

"Ramona and her Mother"

Letter to an Author

Letter writers find that most authors enjoy receiving letters and will write back if the letter is sent in care of their publisher and there is a return address from the writer. It's also great fun to design a postcard around a scene in the book and write a letter on it.

Materials:

Paper and checklist   Pencil/pen

Publisher address   Stamped envelope

Goal:

To write a letter to an author/illustrator

Steps:

1. Look at the Letter Idea Checklist.
2. Check what you want to include in your letter.
3. Find the address of the publisher on the inside of the author's book.
4. Write your letter to the author using the publisher's address and the idea checklist.
5. Include a stamped, self-addressed envelope if you want the author to write back to you.

Letter to an Author Example

November 21, 1992

Mr. Louis Sacher
Avon Books
1350 Ave. of the Americas
New York, NY 10019

Dear Mr. Sacher,

    Hi! My name is Brian Schnierer. I am going to be 9. I live in Woodinville, Washington. These are a couple of questions I would like you to answer please.

    Where do you live? What's your favorite thing to do? When was the first book you made? How old were you when you made your first book? Are you married? How much children do you have? What is your favorite book that you made? Who is your favorite author besides you? Who is your favorite illustrator?

    I put an envelope with my name and address inside so you can write me back. I really like your book Sideways Stories from the Wayside School. Why did you make Todd say he was stupid?

    Please write me back. Thank you.

Brian S.

✓✓✓✓✓✓✓✓✓
Letter Idea Checklist

Things I want to include:

Greeting (Hello, Hi)	❏
Tell something about me	❏
What I like in your book(s)	❏
Tell why I am writing	❏
Possible questions	
Where do you live?	○
Are you married?	○
Do you have children?	○
When did you write your first book?	○
How old were you?	○
Why do you write books?	○
What do you like to write best?	○
What are your writing strengths?	○
What is hard for you to write?	○
What is your favorite book?	○
Who is your favorite author?	○
Who is your favorite illustrator?	○
Who is your favorite character in your books?	○
Specific book questions	❏
Closing (Thank you)	❏
Sign my Name	❏

Name:_____

Author Profile Sheet

It's fun for readers to learn about their favorite authors.

Materials:
Form (copy – page 139)
Pencil/pen

Goal:
To write biographical information about an author

Steps:
1. Go to the library to find out about an author or send a letter with the questions you want answered (see page 40).
2. Write the information you gather in the different folders and graphics.
3. Share your profile with friends who like the author too.

Just for Fun:
Create your own form or use your own headings on a copy of this form
Interview an author in person

Author Profile Example

Name: Jerry Yoo
Date: 1-11-93

(Michelle O'Brien-Palmer)

Michelle
38
woodinvi'l
Wa.

Author's name, age and home

Michelle
Nick
Gid
Sissy (cat)

Author's family

The three books
The books are
Thorgh my eyes
Book write and
Book talk.

Number of books written and some book titles

Poetry and how to write books.

Favorite type of writing

becquse it is crative and fun

Why author likes to write

Illustrator Profile Example

Name: Brandon

Denny
Driver
28

Illustrator's name and age

East
Wenachee,
WA.

Illustrator's home

Denny
Susan
tiffiny
Izac

Illustrator's family

5 Books
Book-write
Book-Talk
Katrina the Butterfly
We like bugs
The African Rain Song

**Number of books illustrated
and some titles**

Graphic
Dezine

Favorite type of art

It's fun!

Why illustrator likes to draw

My Favorite Illustrators Example

Name: SHANNON

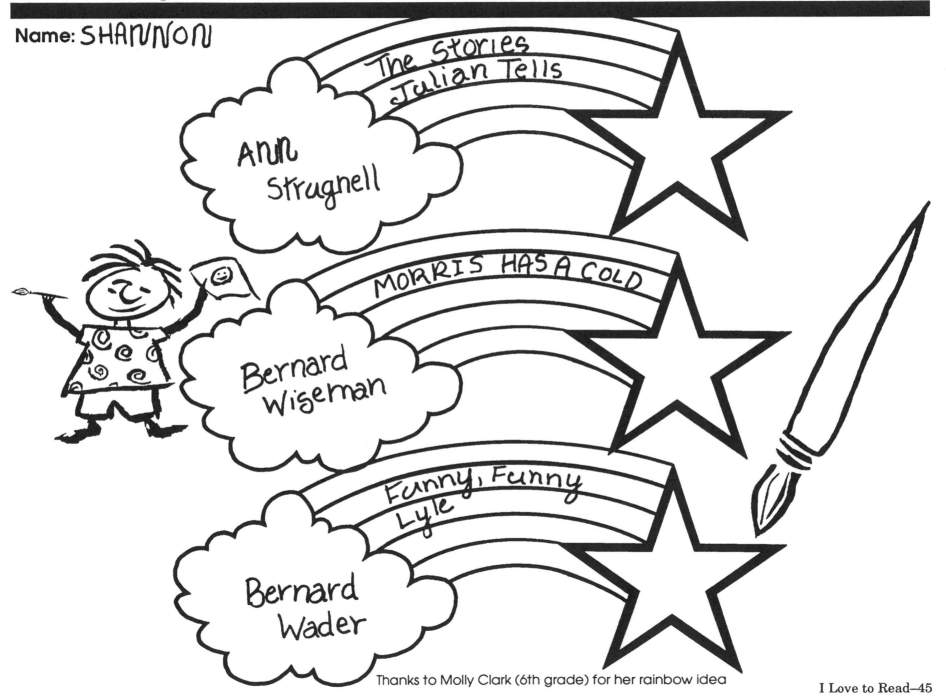

The Stories
Julian Tells

Ann
Strugnell

MORRIS HAS A COLD

Bernard
Wiseman

Funny, Funny
Lyle

Bernard
Wader

Thanks to Molly Clark (6th grade) for her rainbow idea

Chapter 3
Read and Respond

Read and Respond

"I love to read a good book because you just can't stop reading it and you always think about it." Sean Leverentz, 4th grade

Reading is an exciting personal adventure. Each person is touched by a book in a unique way. The experiences you've had in your life, your feelings about different things and what you know about the world influence how you respond to the book you are reading. One of the wonders of reading is a book's ability to pull you into its story. You can become a character; you can experience the book as if you were there.

This chapter presents many different ways to share your book experience with others.

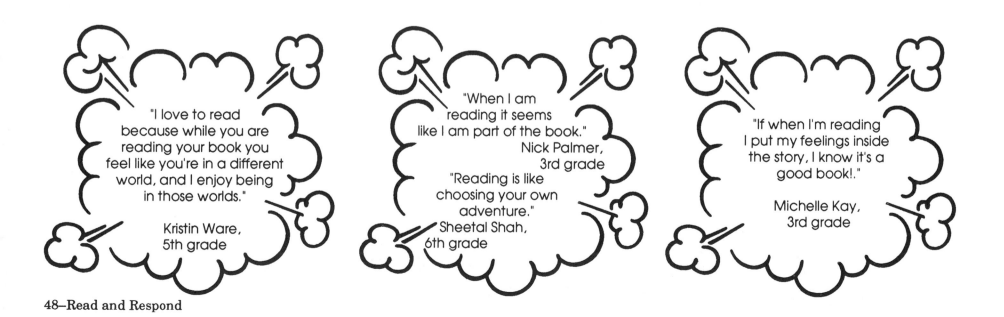

"I love to read because while you are reading your book you feel like you're in a different world, and I enjoy being in those worlds."

Kristin Ware, 5th grade

"When I am reading it seems like I am part of the book." Nick Palmer, 3rd grade
"Reading is like choosing your own adventure." Sheetal Shah, 6th grade

"If when I'm reading I put my feelings inside the story, I know it's a good book!."

Michelle Kay, 3rd grade

About this Chapter

This chapter includes...

Story Sheet

The story sheet helps younger readers respond to the story through three basic but thought-provoking questions (p. 51). It helps them share their story experience.

Predictions

Using a book cover, book title, or first paragraph, readers predict what they think might happen in a story (p. 52). These predictions are based upon their life experience and knowledge. Predicting creates an incredible desire to read the story. Readers enjoy sharing and comparing their predictions.

Response Journal

A journal allows the reader an opportunity to express his or her written response to the book. Response journals can take on many forms, both structured and unstructured. They vary from open-ended writing to the use of topic questions (p. 55).

Story Maps

Story maps help readers recognize and analyze the elements of a story. They provide a structure for talking about a story. This chapter shares three types of maps (p. 57–59).

Retelling

Retelling a story through drawings (p. 60), aloud (p. 62), and writing (p. 64), combines many literacy skills (reading, comprehension, thinking, remembering, organizing information, and communicating through writing). Retelling a story to others can be very empowering.

Comparisons

Readers are asked to identify similarities and differences in their predictions and in the story as written by the author (p. 66), between stories (p. 68) and between characters (p. 70).

Story Sheet

The story sheet provides younger readers with a framework to discuss how they made meaning of a story.

Materials:
Form (copy – page 142)
Pencil/pen/markers

Goal:
To think about things you noticed and felt when you read the story

Steps:
1. In the clouds, write the things you noticed about the story.
2. Circle the faces that match the feelings you had when you read the story.
3. In the thunderbolts, write how the story reminds you of your life.

Just for Fun:
Do the story sheet after someone reads a story to you

Story Sheet Example

Things I noticed in the story

Feelings I had
(Circle the feelings)

Beginning

(The Foot Book by Dr. Seuss)

Luft and rit

Middle

Blake feet and red feet

End

You meet mor and mor Feet

Luft and rit Feet

it's a good Book

Lechelle

How this story reminds me of my life

Predicting Story Outcomes

Predicting makes reading a book even more exciting. After predicting what we think might happen, we are eager to see how our predictions are similar to and different from the story written by the author.

Materials:
Paper
Pencil/pen/markers
Book of your choice

Goal:
To predict what will happen in a story

Steps:
1. Look at the cover, the title, or the first paragraph of the book you want to read.
2. Write your version of the story using the clues you find in the cover, title, or first paragraph (see examples).
3. Read the book to see how the author told the story.

Just for Fun:
Draw the story instead of writing it

Predicting Examples

Prediction: Book Title

Brian Schnierer

Chicken Sunday
by Patricia Polacco

One morning two kids took their mom and dad's cooking stuff out. They took the leftovers which were chicken, hot fudge and vanilla ice cream out of the re-fridgerator. They put it all in the mixer for two minutes. They poured it out in two glasses. One of the kids tried it and said "It's a miracle - it's delicious." The other kid tried it and said "you're right! It is delicious." So they went to a ice cream stand and sold it for $50.00 and they bought a nintendo game.

Prediction: Paragraph

Kaili Ka'lua'hini'nui Jackson

A Christmas Sonata
by Gary Paulsen

What I think is going to happen is that he overhears someone saying how all little kids believe in Santa Claus and how dumb it is.

The small boy hears that and is all sad that Santa Claus may not be real.

Prediction: Cover

It's the Soup that Made Me Sad
Story by Shannon Rubin • Illustrations by John G. Gay

It's the Soup that Made Me Sad
by Shannon Rubin

Steven Yoo

I think whats going to happen is that a girl went to a restrong and when they ordered some soup, the girl thought the bowl was small but when she looked at it, it looked big, its not big, it was huge.

Response Journal

A response journal is a wonderful way to integrate the personal meaning a story has for you through the writing process. Journals can be private or can be shared. Many teachers enjoy responding to each entry. This journal could also be used in conjunction with the literature groups in Chapter 5.

Materials:
Paper
Pencil/pen/markers

Goal:
To record your feelings and thoughts about the story you are reading

Steps:
1. Read in the book you've chosen.
2. Write or draw your thoughts and feelings about the story in your journal.
3. Share these with a friend or teacher.

Just for Fun:
Create your own journal cover and inside pages

Response Journal Example

Phillip
January 15, 1993

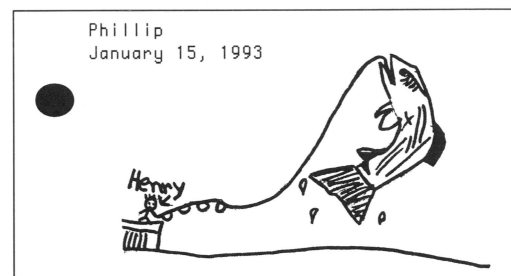

Henry's dad is thinking about takeing Henry fishing. I think Henry will catch a Chinhook. Henry has to keep his dog ribsy out of trouble inorder to go fishing. If I was Henry I would leash ribsy up. I feel that it is hard to keep your dog out of trouble.

This story taught me that if you have to do something give it your best shot.

Story Map

Story mapping helps readers recognize and analyze the elements of the story. A story map can take on many forms (see pages 57-59).

Materials:
Form (copy – page 143)
Paper/pencil/pen

Goal:
To think through the different story elements (characters, setting, problem, solution and conclusion)

Steps:
1. Read your book.
2. Fill in each box on the map.

Just for Fun:
Design your own story map
Create a group story map (see pages 58–59)

Story Map Individual Example

Name: Nick
Title: Helen Keller
Author: Margaret Davidson

Helen Keller
Annie Sullivan
Mr. and Mrs. Keller

CHARACTERS ▲   SETTING ▼

The story takes place in the late 1800's and early 1900's

In Alabama and Boston

PROBLEM(S) ▼

1. Helen got sick and she became blind, deaf and she couldn't talk.

2. Her parents didn't know what to do.

3. No one in her town knew how to communicate with her.

Helen was able to ride horses

She went to college and she got to go to the White House and be in the paper

She became famous

CONCLUSION ▲

SOLUTION(S) ▼

Her parents called Annie Sullivan

She taught Helen how to talk

She taught her to read with her hands and communicate with her hands

She got her into the Perkins School for the Blind

Story Map Group Example

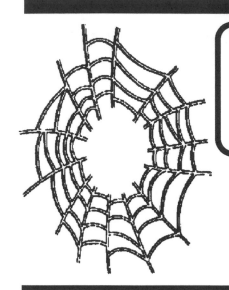

Setting

Chapter 1: Morning time at Arables' Farm
Chapter 2: The Arables' Farm
Chapter 3: Zuckermans' Farm
and so on...

Main Characters

Fern
Wilbur
Charlotte

Supporting Characters

sheep   goose
teacher   pupils
Mr./Mrs. Arables
Lurvy   rooster
Templeton
Mr./Mrs. Zuckerman

Charlotte's Web
by
E.B. White

Vocabulary

runt - small weakling
infant- baby
relieved-- to feel better
hullabaloo-
trough--
peered-- looked
vanished-- disappeared
slops--
and so on...

Chapter Title	Problem	Solution
1 Before Breakfast	Mr. Arable was planning to kill a runt piglet.	Fern stopped her dad and saved the piglet.
2 Wilbur	Wilbur is going to be sold by Mr. Arable	He gets sold to Fern's uncle, Mr. Zuckerman, so she can visit Wilbur.

and so on...

Story map by Lori Blevins Gonwick's 3rd–grade classroom

Story Map Group Example

The Mitten
Jan Brett

Beginning:

Nick lost his mitten. First the mole found a nice cozy place in the mitten. Next the snowshoe rabbit squished in. Then they let the hedgehog in. Then the owl came in the mitten. Then the badger wiggled in too.

Climax:

The fox squished in and finally the bear scrunched in. The mouse got on the bear's nose and he sneezed.

Ending:

Nick found his mitten flying in the air like a bird.

Retelling Through Drawing

Great fun for all ages but especially for non-writers. Retelling has been found to enhance students' reading/listening comprehension. The written description of the drawing example can be found on page 63.

Materials:
Paper
Pencil/pens/markers/crayons

Goal:
To retell a story with pictures

Steps:
1. Listen to or read your story.
2. Draw one picture or a group of pictures that tell the story.

Just for Fun:
Draw pictures to express your <u>feelings</u> as you listened to the story

Retelling Example

Goldilocks and the Three Bears, Retold by Lissa Rubin
(Written description on page 63)

Retelling Aloud

It is very exciting for non-readers first to retell stories with pictures and then to use their drawings to retell the story aloud in their own words. Having another person write down what they say is also very validating.

Materials:
Paper
Pencil/pens

Goals:
To retell a story
To remember the story through your own
  drawings of it

Step:
1. Look at your story pictures.
2. Tell what happens in each picture.

Just for Fun:
Have someone write your words onto paper
Tape record the story as you retell it
Have someone videotape you as you retell
  the story

Retelling Example

1. Once upon a time there was a little cottage and there was 3 windows. There was really 4 but one of them went to the kitchen and there was 4 dots on each one cause that's how you pull the window parts out.

2. Three bears lived in that place and they went to get some honey. And there was a Papa Bear, Mama Bear and a Baby Bear. They went out to get some honey.

3. Then this little girl came. She saw the little cottage and then there was dark clouds. And so she had to get into the cottage really fast.

4. So she got into the cottage and found a table. She saw 3 bowls and 3 cups. She first tried the Papa Bear's cereal - it was too hot, then the Mama Bear's - it was too cold. Then she tried the Baby Bear's - it was just right.

5. Then she went upstairs and found 3 beds. She tried the Papa Bear's - it was too hard, the Mama Bear's was too soft. She tried the Baby Bear's bed and

6. it was just right – so she went to sleep.

7. When the 3 bears came home

8. they went into their rooms and checked their beds. The Papa Bear said "Somebody was sleeping in my bed." The Mama Bear said "Somebody was sleeping in my bed." The Baby Bear said "and she's still there."

9. Goldilocks jumped out of bed and ran downstairs as fast as she could and she didn't know how to unlock it. She found that wood piece, picked it up, ran outside and peeked in the gate, shook it - it was locked.

10. And then there was a policeman and he opened the gate for her and he walked her to her house.

(Dictated by Lissa using her drawings on page 61)

Retelling Through Writing

Retelling combines many literacy skills: reading, comprehension, thinking, remembering, organizing information and communicating through writing.

Materials:
Paper
Pencil/pen

Goal:
To retell a story

Step:
1. Read your book.
2. Be sure that you really understand what you've read.
3. Without looking at the book, pretend you are writing the story down for a friend who hasn't read it, and that you want him to enjoy it as much as you did.
4. Write the story in your own words onto your paper.

Just for Fun:
Write a letter to a friend retelling the story

Retelling Examples

Retelling

Brian
Chicken Sunday
P.Polacco

A Grandmother named Miss Eula makes chicken dinner every Sunday and wants a special hat she can't buy. Her grandsons and the girl telling the story want to buy her that hat but they have to pay Mr. Kodinski. They don't have enough money so they paint eggs. Mr. Kodinski likes them and the kids sell them at his store. He gives them the pink hat for Miss Eula. She was real happy.

Retelling

Name: Kaili
Book Title: A Christmas Sonata
Book Author: Kaili

The story is about a boy who see's a neighbor in a Santa outfit and thinks that there isn't a real Santa.

He gets really sad and is mad at his mom and dad. He thinks that there is no real meaning to Christmas. Then when he is with his dying cousin on Christmas Eve night the small boys Uncle Ben is reading a story when he says he heard bells. They run outside and they see four real reindeer and one real Santa. The small boys believed in him from then on.

Retelling

Steven
It's the Soup that Made Me Sad by Shannon Rubin

Kimi's room was a mess and she couldn't find her baseball mitt so she couldn't play.
Then her dad called they're going out to dinner. When Kimi went out of her bed she tripped over the mitt and she said "stupid mitt."
Then they were at the restaurant and her mother said "what do you want for dinner" and she said "just soup." Then the soup came and when she looked at the soup it wasn't plain, it was big. It was huge. Everything in the soup made Kimi sad. She ate everything one by one.

Then she went to her room and picked stuff up one by one. And Kimi called her parents and told them that she cleaned up the mess.

Predicting Comparisons

Once a story has been retold, the reader can then analyze the similarities and differences between her prediction and the story as written by the author.

Materials:
Prediction sheet
Retelling sheet
Paper
Pencil/pens

Goal:
To compare your prediction with the story as written by the author

Steps:
1. Re-read your completed book prediction and story retell.
2. Using the questions above or the comparison forms (p. 69–70) identify the similarities and differences between your prediction and retell.

Predicting Comparison Examples

It's the Soup that Made Me Sad
Comparison by Steven

Prediction
Kimi was at the restaurant the whole time.

soup was huge in restaurant

Story
Kimi's room was a mess.

She missed baseball game

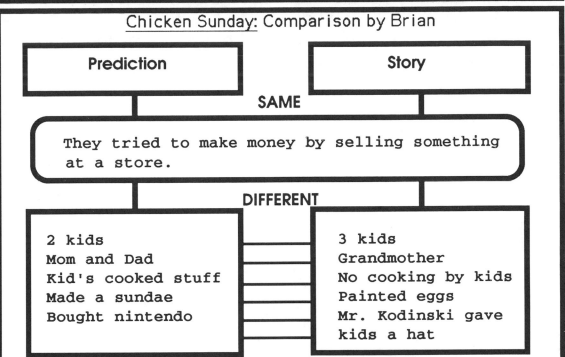

Prediction		Story

SAME

They tried to make money by selling something at a store.

DIFFERENT

2 kids Mom and Dad Kid's cooked stuff Made a sundae Bought nintendo	3 kids Grandmother No cooking by kids Painted eggs Mr. Kodinski gave kids a hat

A Christmas Sonata
Comparison by Kaili

Prediction		**Story**
Small boy overhears someone say that there was no Santa. He's really sad	The small boy thinks that Santa isn't real.	He saw a fake Santa drinking wine. He learned the true meaning of Christmas through his cousin.

Comparison Sheets

The Venn Diagram (p. 69) and Character Comparison Sheet (p.70) both provide the opportunity to compare and contrast various elements in a story. Try comparing two books, a movie and book, two characters or two versions of the same story.

Materials:
Forms (copy – page 144 and 145)
Pencil/pens

Goal:
To compare two stories or characters

Steps:
1. Read your story/stories.
2. In the middle shape, write the things the stories/characters have in common.
3. In each outside shape, write the differences between the two stories/characters.

Just for Fun:
Use two balloon shapes (see page 67)

Venn Diagram Example

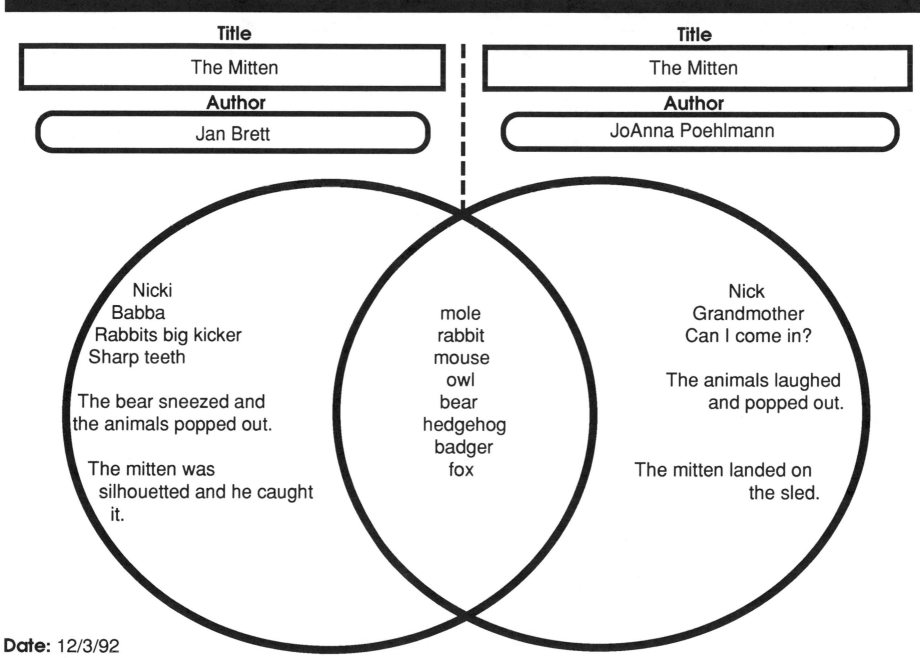

Title

The Mitten

Author

Jan Brett

Title

The Mitten

Author

JoAnna Poehlmann

Nicki
Babba
Rabbits big kicker
Sharp teeth

The bear sneezed and
the animals popped out.

The mitten was
  silhouetted and he caught
  it.

mole
rabbit
mouse
owl
bear
hedgehog
badger
fox

Nick
Grandmother
Can I come in?

The animals laughed
and popped out.

The mitten landed on
  the sled.

Date: 12/3/92
Name: Suzie Fiebig's 2nd-grade classroom

Character Comparison Example

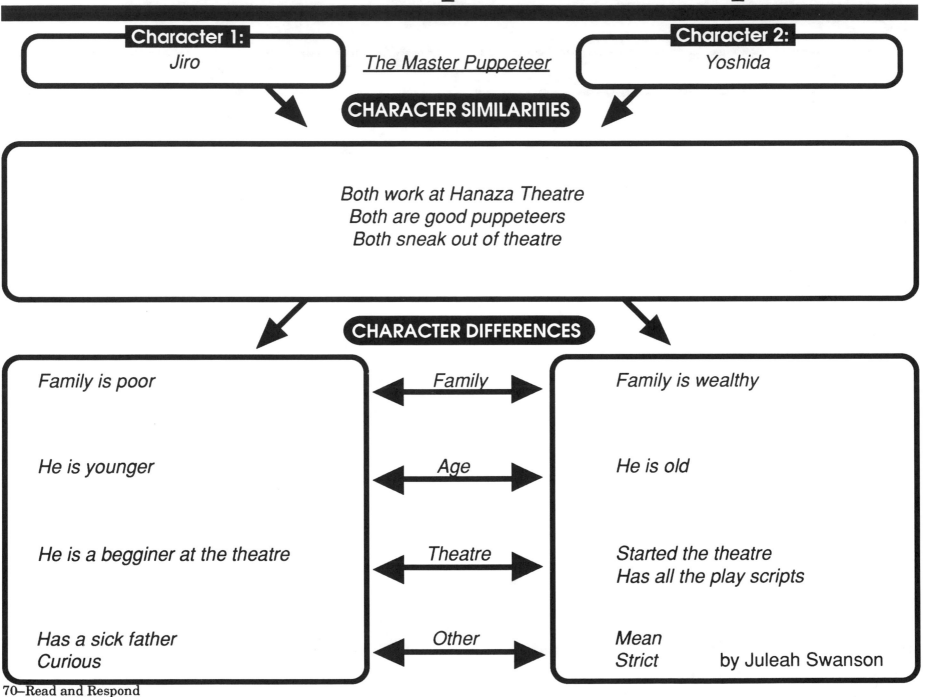

Character 1: Jiro

The Master Puppeteer

Character 2: Yoshida

CHARACTER SIMILARITIES

Both work at Hanaza Theatre
Both are good puppeteers
Both sneak out of theatre

CHARACTER DIFFERENCES

Jiro		Yoshida
Family is poor	Family	Family is wealthy
He is younger	Age	He is old
He is a begginer at the theatre	Theatre	Started the theatre Has all the play scripts
Has a sick father Curious	Other	Mean Strict by Juleah Swanson

Chapter 4

Read and Review

Read and Review

As we read a book, we evaluate (judge) it many times. If it captures our interest we are drawn into the story. Many people have difficulty putting a great book down. If it doesn't capture our attention we may lose interest and put it aside. If the story doesn't make sense to us or we don't understand what is going on, we feel frustrated.

There are many ways to review a book. As with reading, reviewing a book is very personal. We each evaluate a book through our own interests and personal experience of it. Reviewing a book means determining what you thought of the book, how you liked it, how much of a challenge it was to you, and whether or not you would recommend it to a friend.

Book reviews can be written or given orally (out loud). Book-Sells (p.74) and Book-Talks (p.76) are usually oral. Pizza Reports (p. 86) and Remarkable Reviewer Reviews (p. 83-85) are written.

When you review a book, you share your reading experience with others. **Your opinion is very important and may help others in selecting their next books.**

"A good book is a book I like to read because it's fun to read and exciting."

Ed Lobdell, 1st grade

"I like books to have a happy ending and a good starting and things that I like in them."

Tiffany Driver, 2nd grade

"I think a book's really good when the author puts excitement into the book and shows a character's talent ."

Gavin Schroder, 4th grade

"A good book is one that interests you, that keeps your attention and makes you want to read on."

Emily Mack, 5th grade

About This Chapter

This chapter includes...

Oral Book Reviews

Oral Review Evaluations

Self Evaluations

Buddy Evaluations

Written Book Reviews

Book-Sell

Kids love to do book-sells. They are eager to do them after watching the public television spot "Reading Rainbow." See page 78 and page 80 for the evaluation component.

Materials:

Paper	Checklist
Pencil	Book
Video camera	Reading Rainbow TV Show

Goal:
To persuade others to read your book

Steps:
1. Watch several "Reading Rainbow" TV shows (usually on PBS in the afternoon).
2. Note some book-sell ideas from "Reading Rainbow" kids (your favorite slogans etc.)
3. Use the checklist (p. 75) to include all the information you want in your book-sell.
4. Write your book-sell draft.
5. Practice with a friend and make revisions.
6. Have someone videotape your book-sell.

Book-Sell Examples

A Book-Sell

- [ ] **Your Name**
- [ ] **Book Title, Author, Illustrator**
- [ ] **Genre** (type of book)
- [ ] **Character(s)**
- [ ] **Problem(s)**
- [ ] **How you feel about this book**
- [ ] **Something interesting about the story** (but don't give the ending away!)
- [ ] **Invite the audience to READ THIS BOOK!**

Nick

Book-Sell

Hi! My name is Nick. I just read a great book called "Helen Keller." It's a true story.

Can you imagine what it would be like to always be in the dark and never hear a sound? Can you imagine not communicating with other people? Well, that's what Helen Keller's life was like.

Find out how Helen was helped by her friend Annie and became famous. Read this great book!

Steven

Book-Sell

Hi! My name is Steven Yoo. I just read "It's the Soup That Made Me Sad." I really liked it.

Kimi has a problem. Her room is a mess and she can't find her baseball mitt. So she can't go to the game with her friends.

To see how a huge bowl of soup helps Kimi to clean up her room, you've got to read this book!

Book-Talk

A book-talk is usually given by more experienced readers. When preparing for a book-talk, it helps to look at presentation content and style separately (see page 77). Thanks to Sue Parker (6th-grade teacher) for her evaluation ideas.

Materials:

Checklists on page 77   Paper

Pencil   Book

Goal:

To share the book you just read with others

Steps:

1. Think about what you find interesting in book-talks (content). Write it down.
2. Think about what makes a speaker interesting (style) to you. Write it down.
3. Using the content checklist (p.77), select the content items you want to include in your book-talk.
4. Write your draft book-talk.
5. Re-read your style notes and style checklist on page 77.
6. Practice with a friend and revise.
7. Give your book-talk.

Book-Talk Checklist and Example

Book-Talk Content Checklist ✔

Name:

Things I want to include in my Book-Talk:

1
- ☐ Book Title, Author, Illustrator
- ☐ Genre
- ☐ Visual about the book (see Chapter)
- ☐ My challenge level low 1•2•3•4•5 high
- ☐ Catchy opening statement
  (tell something interesting)

2
- ☐ What attracted me to the book
- ☐ Short problem summary
- ☐ What I liked/didn't like
- ☐ Overall rating 1-10
- ☐ The changes I'd make to the story

3
- ☐ Other books by this author
- ☐ Information about the author
- ☐ Information about the illustrator
- ☐ Snappy closing summary
- ☐ Would I recommend this book?(Why?)

Book-Talk Style Checklist
- ☐ Eye Contact --------------Look at your audience
- ☐ Voice -----------------------Speak slowly, clearly
- ☐ Voice -----------------------Speak loudly enough
- ☐ Enthusiasm ----------------High energy level

Juleah

My Book-Talk

The Master Puppeteer is an awsome book. It was written by Katherine Paterson who has won two Newberry Awards. The illustrator, Haru Wells animated some cartoons for Sesame Street. I chose the book because it's a Newberry Award winner and it takes place in Japan with a Japanisse heritage. I like this book because it is a mixture book. It is sad, happy, part mystery, and very good. The book could also be the Japinisse version of Robin Hood because a mysterious man steals from the rich and gives to the poor or hungry. Jiro, the main character, wants to know who the mysterious man (Saburo) is. Saburo has appeared at many places, even Hanza Puppet Theatre, but no one has ever seen him.

I learned about puppeteering in Japan. Puppeteering sounds fun and hard. I would like to try it some day. I think the author wrote it because it is such an interesting subject. Some changes I would make are making Saburo come up more in the beginning, and make it more a mystery.

Other books by Katherine Paterson are Bridge to Terrbithia, and The Sign of the Chrysanthemum. I hope you read The Master Puppeteer and enjoy it as much as I did.

Book-Sell Self-Evaluation Form

My Book-Sell

Name:
Book Title:
Book Author:

1. How did you like doing your book-sell? Please explain.

2. How did you feel watching your book-talk videotape? Please explain.

3. Do you think your book-sell was interesting? Yes ☐   No ☐

4. If you could change something about your book-sell, what would it be?

Book-Talk Self-Evaluation Form

My Book-Talk Self-Evaluation

Book Title:
Book Author:

My Rating Scale
Need practice   Met my goal
1•2•3•4•5

Was I interesting? -- 1•2•3•4•5 CONTENT
Did my opening catch my audience's attention? ---- 1•2•3•4•5
Did I pique my audience's interest? -------------------- 1•2•3•4•5
Did I tell too much about the story? ------------------ 1•2•3•4•5
Did I have a good closing statement? ---------------- 1•2•3•4•5
Did I mention other books by this author? ------------ 1•2•3•4•5

Did I have eye contact with my audience? ----------- 1•2•3•4•5   STYLE
How was my voice quality? ----------------------------- 1•2•3•4•5
Was my visual presentation bright and colorful? ------ 1•2•3•4•5
Did I show enthusiasm for my book? ------------------ 1•2•3•4•5
The part I liked best about my book-talk was:

In my next book-talk, the one thing I am going to work on will be:

Signed_____

Book-Sell Buddy Review Form

Book-Sell Buddy Review

Date:
Presenter's Name: _____
Book Title: _____

1. Do you want to read this book now? Yes ☐ No ☐ Why?

2. What was your favorite part of the book-sell? Please explain.

3. Do you think the book-sell was interesting? Yes ☐ No ☐

Signed _____

Book-Talk Buddy Review Form

Book-Talk Buddy Review

Date:
Name of Presenter:
Name of Book:

The things I really liked in your book-talk:

Ideas for future book-talks:

Signed _____

Book-Talk Buddy Review

Rating Scale
Needs practice   Great job
1•2•3•4•5

Content
Kept my interest ------------------- 1•2•3•4•5
Catchy opening ----------------- 1•2•3•4•5
Story information ---------------- 1•2•3•4•5
Author information -------------- 1•2•3•4•5
Closing summary ---------------- 1•2•3•4•5

Style
Eye contact ---------------------- 1•2•3•4•5
Voice quality -------------------- 1•2•3•4•5
Visual presentation quality ------ 1•2•3•4•5
Book enthusiasm ---------------- 1•2•3•4•5

After hearing this book-talk are you interested in reading this book? Yes ☐ No ☐
Why?

Remarkable Reviewer Reviews

The Remarkable Reviewer sheets can be used once a reader is familiar with the different elements in a story and feels comfortable with evaluating a book. Depending on the evaluation, a book will fall into one of three categories: hot, not hot, or OK. This helps categorize books for others who may be interested in a certain title.

Materials:
Forms (copy – page 146, 147, and 148)
Paper/pencil/pen

Goals:
To review the book you just read
To share your review with others

Steps:
1. Read your book.
2. Decide the category your book fits into: Hot, Not Hot, or OK.
3. Answer the questions on the sheet that fits your book.
4. Share your review with friends.

Just for Fun:
Design your own review form(s)
Create notebooks for each category

Remarkable Reviewer

This Book's HOT!

Name: Shannon Bovan

Title
The Stories Julian Tells

Author
Ann Cameron

Illustrator
Ann Strugnell

Characters
Julian
Gloria

Setting

Not
Sure

Summary of Story

The dad spends like an hour making pudding for the mom and used like twenty lemons and a dozen and a half eggs. And the kids eat it all and hid under the bed. The dad comes in and sees the goop on the floor.

I chose this book because: <u>I liked the names of the stories. One was eating lemon pudding their dad was making for their mom's birthday.</u>

My favorite part of this book was: <u>When the kids get in trouble from their dad for eating their moms pudding and they hid under the bed.</u>

Remarkable Reviewer

This Book's NOT HOT!

Name: Kaili

My Challenge Scale
Low 1 • 2 • 3 • ④ • 5 High

Title
Where the Red Fern Grows

Author
Wilson Rawls

Illustrator

Short Summary

A boy gets two puppies that are hunting dogs. He takes them out for hunting. One got killed in the beginning of hunting and the next got killed too. The dogs were buried at his house. When he had to move he didn't want to because his dogs were still there. Then a red fern grows in between the place where the two dogs are buried. It was an Indian symbol and then he felt better about moving.

I chose this book because: Someone said it was a good book.

I didn't like this book because: It was really gross and sad. One part: this boy falls on an axe and the author discribes it very clearly. The boy has blood bubles coming out of his mouth (that is just one of gross seens). Then the dogs (2 dogs) die and the author discribes that very clearly: I also hate any book that has a pet dieing.

Remarkable Reviewer

This Book is <u>OK</u>

My Challenge Scale
Low 1 • 2 •③• 4 • 5 High

Name: Terry Yoo

Title
Harriet Tubman

Author
Kate McMullan

Illustrator
Steven James

Characters
Harriet Tubman
John Tubman
Harriet's friends   Slaves

Setting
At her house

Plot Summary

Sometimes she is a slave. She rescued over 300 slaves. She got something from Queen Victoria. Harriet got something from a famous person. Harriet Tubman is a famous person. She got into a lot of adventures.

I chose this book because: <u>It was a famous person book.</u>

I think this book is just OK because: <u>I like books about boys better.</u>

I would recommend it to a friend: ☑YES ☐ NO
Please explain: <u>I think it is a good book but not my favorite kind of book.</u>

Pizza Reports

Great evaluation tool for younger readers. Readers start with the Canadian bacon report for the first book, sausage for the next, and so on. By the fourth review, they have discussed setting and main characters, identified goals and summarized a plot. For each completed review, a paper topping can be placed onto a large pizza shape. A full pizza means a pizza party to celebrate reading. Thanks to Lori Blevins Gonwick, for her pizza report ideas.

Materials:
Forms (copy – page 149,150)
Pencil
Pizza bulletin board

Goals:
To write about the different parts of the book you just finished reading
To earn toppings to put on a pizza board

Steps:
1. Make a pizza shape for a bulletin board.
2. After reading your book, answer the questions in report one (report #2 for next book).
3. Make a paper topping to go on the board.
4. Agree upon the number of toppings needed to complete the pizza.
5. When the board is filled with toppings, have a pizza party to celebrate reading.

Pizza Report Examples

Report 1: Setting Identification

Name:

Canadian Bacon Report

_____

Title of the book

Author_____

Illustrator_____

# of pages ___ easy☐ medium☐ challenge☐

Where does the story take place?

_____

_____

_____

Do you recommend this book? Y N

Draw a picture of the setting
on the back

Report 2: Plot Identification

Name:

Sausage Report

Title _____

Author_____ Illustrator_____

# of pages ___ easy☐ medium☐ challenge☐

What happens at the beginning of the story?_____

_____

What happens in the middle of the story?_____

_____

What happens at the end of the story? _____

_____

Do you like the ending?   Yes ☐ No ☐

Report 3: Story Summary

Name:

Anchovy Report

Title_____

Author_____Illustrator_____

# of pages ___   Easy☐ Medium☐ Challenge☐

Write a paragraph about the story. Be sure to
talk about the characters, setting and ending.

_____

_____

_____

_____

Do you recommend
this book? Yes ☐ No ☐

Report 4: Main Character/Goal Identification

Name:

Pepperoni Report

Title_____ .

Author_____

Illustrator_____

# of pages ___ easy☐ medium☐ challenge☐

What is the "Main Character's" goal?

_____

Do you like the "Main Character"? Why?

_____

If you were the "Main Character" what
other ways would you try to reach the
goal?_____

_____

Re-write the ending on
the back

Bubble Gum Review Example

Name: Nick

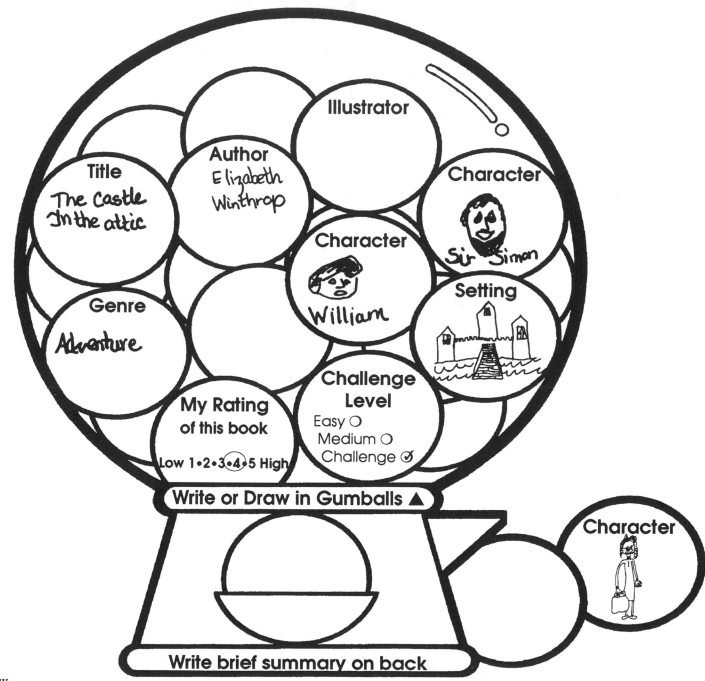

Illustrator

Author
Elizabeth
Winthrop

Title
The Castle
In the attic

Character
Sir Simon

Character
William

Genre
Adventure

Setting

My Rating
of this book

Low 1•2•3•4•5 High

Challenge
Level
Easy ○
Medium ○
Challenge ✓

Write or Draw in Gumballs ▲

Character

Write brief summary on back

Chapter 5

Literature Groups:
Getting Started

Literature Groups

Sharing is a very enjoyable part of reading. This chapter is dedicated to sharing books in literature groups. Literature groups are sometimes called literature circles because the group takes place in a circle. There are usually five to seven members in a group. When a group first starts, it is helpful to have an adult leader get the group going. Later, many groups meet on their own.

Literature groups can share books in a variety of ways. This chapter provides starter questions for three ways to share books: books of the same genre, books by the same author, and story elements of the same book. However, the discussion possibilities are limitless as each unique literature group takes form.

This chapter also includes an evaluation component for literature group members and leaders.

"I think literature circles are fun because I really like books and I really like to talk to other kids about them."
Brian Schnierer
3rd grade

"I like literature groups where the kids are really nice, listen to you, and are excited about their books."
Kasi Farrar
4th grade

"A fun literature group is where you have kids who pay attention, have read the book, and ask interesting questions."
Savahn Rosinbum
5th grade

About this Chapter

This chapter includes...

Book Selection

Two techniques for literature group book selection are presented:

Book Club Circle

Book Club Circles help younger readers share their books in a fun, relaxed manner. Very basic questions are asked to help ease them into book discussions.

Literature Groups–Starter Questions:

Directions for possible ways of starting a literature group are included. You will also find Group Starter Questions for genre (page 99), author style (page 103), and story elements (page 101).

Evaluation Component

Book-Share

The book ballot helps readers feel they have a choice in book selection. Many teachers track choices to ensure a first choice at least one out of three times.

Materials:
Book Ballot (copy – page 152)
5-7 copies of each book title
Pencil
Ballot box   Passages from 5 books

Goal:
To select the book you want to read and
  discuss in a literature group

Steps:
1. Listen as a passage from each book is read.
2. Mark your first, second and third book
   choice on the book ballot.
3. Place your ballot in the ballot box.

Just for Fun:
Create your own ballot
Create your own ballot box

Book Ballot Example

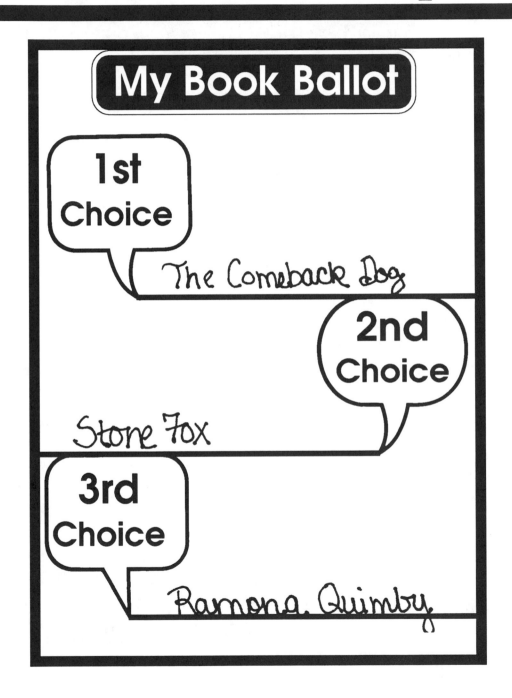

My Book Ballot

1st Choice — The Comeback Dog

2nd Choice

Stone Fox

3rd Choice

Ramona Quimby

Book Exchange

Readers really enjoy participating in a book exchange. It gives them an opportunity to preview a number of books. Many times they find new authors and titles for their Reading Idea List (page 33).

Materials:
Form (copy – page 152)
Pencil
Several copies of many books

Goal:
To select a book for a literature group by previewing many books

Steps:
1. Select your first book.
2. Read for five minutes.
3. Fill out the Book Exchange Notes sheet for books you are interested in reading.
4. Exchange books with someone else.
5. Repeat the process until you have previewed four or five books.
6. Write your first, second and third choice in the choice # box.

Book Exchange Notes Example

Book Exchange Notes

Choice # _2_

Book Title: The Lion, Witch and Wardrobe
Book Author: C.S. Lewis
Genre:
- ☑ Adventure
- ☐ Biography
- ☐ Fantasy
- ☐ Mystery
- ☐ Non-Fiction
- ☐ Realistic Fiction
- ☐ Other:

My Interest Level: Low 1 • 2 • 3 • ④ • 5 High
Notes: I really liked this book

Choice # _1_

Book Title: The Whipping Boy
Book Author: Sid Fleishman
Genre:
- ☑ Adventure
- ☐ Biography
- ☐ Fantasy
- ☐ Mystery
- ☐ Non-Fiction
- ☐ Realistic Fiction
- ☑ Other: Humor

My Interest Level: Low 1 • 2 • 3 • 4 • ⑤ High
Notes: It's interesting and funny too.

Starting a Book Club Circle

The Book Club Circles help younger readers share their book experience with others in a fun, nurturing environment. Adult leadership is necessary to model desired behavior. Circles can also focus on group members sharing their favorite books.

Materials:

5 copies of each book   Chairs in circle

Journal   Pencil

Goal:

To start a book club circle

Steps for first circle:

1. Sit in a circle (5 kids) with others who are going to read the same book.
2. Members share why they chose this book and/or what they think might happen in the story.
3. Members decide how many pages to read for the next meeting (goal).

After first circle:

1. Read your book.
2. Draw a picture or write a sentence in your journal about the story so far.
3. Bring your journal to the next book club to help you talk about the book.

Fun Book Club Starter Questions

Book Club Session 1. Starter Questions

1. What did you like about the cover of this book?
2. Why did you choose this book?
3. What do you think might happen in this story?

Book Club Session 2. Starter Questions

1. What did you notice about this book as you were reading it?
2. Would you like to share your journal drawing or writing?
3. How do you like the story so far? Why?

Book Club Session 3. Starter Questions

1. How did you feel when you were reading the story? (i.e. glad, happy, sad, mad)
2. Would you like to share your journal entry with us?
3. Who is your favorite character?

Book Club Session 4. Starter Questions

1. How does this story remind you of your life?
2. What is your favorite part of the story so far?
3. Please share your journal entry. Tell us about it.

Literature Group Focus: Genre

For brief genre descriptions, see page 21. It helps to start a literature group focused on a certain genre with discussion about the elements of the genre. An adult usually leads the group initially. However, in a short period of time, the adult can take a back seat as group members eagerly discuss their books among themselves. The starter questions are only springboards for future discussion.

Materials:
5-7 books (same genre)   Genre tree (p. 20)
Starter questions (p. 99)   Butcher paper

Goal:
To talk about the elements of a certain genre

Steps:
1. Meet in a group with other people reading a book of the same genre.
2. Brainstorm the elements found in the genre (e.g. Mystery: crime, suspense, climax). Write them onto butcher paper.
3. Members share why they chose their book.
4. Members share their favorite elements in this genre.
5. Members discuss the focus for next group.

Group Starter Questions: Genre

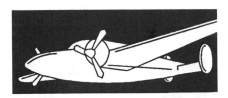

Adventure
1. Briefly tell about the adventure in this story.
2. What parts of the adventure would you like to experience?
3. How would you change the adventure?

Biography
1. Who is the main character? Tell a little about him or her.
2. What new information have you learned about her/him?
3. Do you like this person? Please explain.

Fantasy or Fairytale
1. Where does this story take place?
2. Who is your favorite character? Why?
3. What is your favorite part of the story? Please explain.

Mystery
1. Was a crime committed in the story? If so, what was it?
2. Did the author do a good job building suspense? Please explain.
3. How would you change the mystery?

Historical
1. When does this story take place? Is it fiction or non-fiction?
2. Why were you interested in this time period?
3. Are you like any of the characters? How?

Realistic Fiction
1. Who are the main characters?
2. How does this story remind you of your life?
3. Do you think this story could really happen? Please explain.

Literature Group Focus: Story Elements

Story elements as discussion starters can be used in all types of literature groups. It helps to have an adult lead the group early on and then let the group follow its own direction. Try creating your own group discussion starter questions and then watch how the discussion takes on a life of its own.

Materials:
5-7 copies of the same book
Starter questions (page 101)

Goal:
To discuss story elements in the same book

Steps for first group:
1. Meet in a group with other people reading the same book.
2. Brainstorm the basic elements of any story (i.e. setting, plot, etc.).
3. Members share what first attracted them to the book.
4. Members predict what will happen in the story.
5. Members discuss the focus for the next group.

Group Starter Questions: Story Elements

Prediction
1. What clues does the book cover give you about the story?
2. After reading the first paragraph what do you predict will happen?
3. How does the author try to pull you into the story? Does it work?

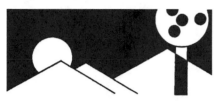
Setting
1. Describe the setting of the story and the time period.
2. Does the setting remind you of anywhere you have been?
3. Do you think the setting fits the story? Why?

Characters
1. Who are the main characters?
2. Who is your favorite character? What makes this character your favorite?
3. What things do you have in common with the characters?

Plot
1. What problems do the characters face? How are they solved?
2. How would you solve these problems? Please explain.
3. Does this story plot remind you of any other story you've read?

Conclusion
1. Did the ending make sense to you? Why?
2. If you could change the ending, how would you change it?
3. If you could write a sequel, what would happen next?

Mood
1. Describe a scene in the book that made you laugh. What was funny?
2. Describe a sad scene. Did it remind you of anything you've experienced?
3. What was the most exciting part of the book? How did it make you feel?

Literature Group Focus: Authors

As readers compare and contrast the writing of different authors, it is a perfect opportunity to integrate what they learn into their own writing.

Materials:
Markers
Starter questions (page 101)
5-7 long rectangular strips of tagboard
5-7 books by different authors

Goal:
To compare the writing of different authors

Steps for first group:
1. Meet in your group.
2. Members write the first sentence in their book onto the tagboard.
3. Members share their sentences.
4. Members discuss the differences and similarities in the first lines. Do these lines make you want to read more? Does one line do this better than another? Why?
5. Members discuss the focus for the next group.

Group Starter Questions: Authors

About this Author

1. What other books have you read by this author?
2. What do you know about this author?
3. How did you first learn about his/her books?

Genre

1. Does this author always write in the same genre?
2. Why do you think this author writes the books he/she does?
3. Do you like this person's writing? Please explain.

Research

1. Do you think this author does research to write his/her books?
2. What kinds of things did the author have to know to write this book?
3. How long do you think it would take to write this story?

Interest Level

1. Why did you choose to read this book?
2. How did the author capture your interest in the beginning of the story?
3. Has the author been able to keep you interested? How?

Language

1. Does the author do a good job of painting pictures with words?
2. What are your favorite passages so far?
3. Do you like the way the author describes the setting, characters and events? Give examples.

Story Line

1. Does the story make sense?
2. Has the author done a good job of explaining things in the story?
3. How would you change the way the story is written?

Literature Group Self-Evaluation

Although literature groups take on many forms (structured and unstructured), they all present an opportunity to self-assess behavior and learning in a group setting. You will find a literature group assesment tool for teachers or parents on page 106. Thanks to Martha Ivy (4th-grade teacher) for her evaluation ideas.

Materials:
Form (copy–page 153)
Pencil/pen

Goals:
To assess how well you met your group goals
To record what you learned in your literature
 group

Steps:
1. Write today's date on the form.
2. Write your group's goal for this meeting.
3. Fill in whether or not you met this goal.
4. Record what you learned in the group.
5. Give yourself a +, ✓ or – for your effort
   and participation.

Literature Group Self-Evaluation Example

Date	Our group goal for today was:	Met goal Yes	No	In my literature group today I learned...	+ ✓ − I give myself a
2/1	no goal yet	✓		the parts of a mystery	+ ☺
2/8	read Chapter 1	✓		about foreshadowing	+ ☺
2/16	read Chapter 2		✓	I didn't feel good	still sick
2/23	read Chpt. 3	✓		suspense building	✓
3/2	READ CHPT. 4	✓		Story Climax- Stuff	+

Literature Group Record Keeping

yellow grp. 3-2-93

Student's Name	Preparation			Participation: low 1•2•3 high			
	Brought Book	Read Book	Noted his/her Interests	In group	Response Quality	Text Reference	Listening Skills
John P.	✓	✓	—	didn't talk much · 2	a bit distracted · 1	yes · 2	OK · 2
Sara M.	✓	✓	✓	very talkative · 3	very thoughtful · 3	yes- a lot · 3	very interested · 3
Tara N.	✓	✓	✓	some · 2	Prepared well · 3	yes- a lot · 3	More interested in talking · 2
Brandon C.	✓	—	—	Did not talk much · 2	wasn't feeling well · 2	no · 1	very interested · 3
Tony L.	✓	✓	✓	very talkative · 3	Great · 3	many times · 3	Great interest · 3

Notes:

New group, just getting started.
Learning appropriate group behaviors
Overall - doing very well

Chapter 6
Fun Reading Projects

Fun Reading Projects

"My favorite reading project is a Wanted Poster. It's fun making up what the people did right or wrong and it's fun drawing." Kelsey Holt, 5th grade

Readers are inspired in different ways by the stories they've read. Reading a good book can be very energizing. It's fun to use that energy to create something that symbolizes what we've read. It's a wonderful opportunity to extend our reading experience.

The reading projects in this chapter are based upon the recommendations of other kids. They were asked to share their classroom favorites with *Book-Talk* readers. The projects that are included in this chapter are those they felt were the most fun to create and share with others. Each project has been kid-tested and approved.

We hope you enjoy these projects. **Have fun creating your own reading projects!**

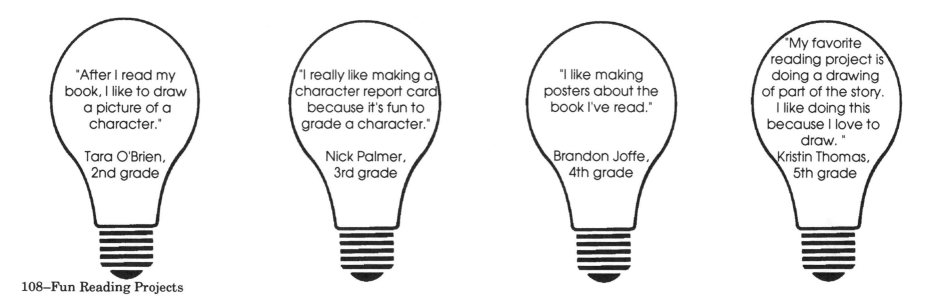

"After I read my book, I like to draw a picture of a character."

Tara O'Brien, 2nd grade

"I really like making a character report card because it's fun to grade a character."

Nick Palmer, 3rd grade

"I like making posters about the book I've read."

Brandon Joffe, 4th grade

"My favorite reading project is doing a drawing of part of the story. I like doing this because I love to draw. "
Kristin Thomas, 5th grade

About This Chapter

This chapter includes...

Reading Project List

The Reading Project List on page 155, includes the name and page number of twenty reading projects listed throughout *Book-Talk*. It provides ideas for readers who are interested in doing a reading project and a place to record a completed project.

Projects in this Chapter

The projects in this chapter help readers synthesize and apply what they have learned from the books they've read. The following projects are included:

Special Bookmarks	page 112	Puppet Characters	page 114
Character Report Card	page 116	Story Cube	page 119
Story Quilt	page 120	Character Mask	page 120
Character Wanted Poster	page 124	Setting Map	page 126
Advertise-a-Book Poster	page 128		

The Project Supply Sheet on page 130, helps readers organize their project materials.

Reading Project List

The Reading Project List helps readers keep track of the various projects they've already completed. It also helps them select a reading project . The Project Supply Sheet on page 130 will help readers organize their projects.

Materials:
Form (copy – page 155)
Pencil/pen

Goals:
To record the projects you've completed and their book titles
To help you select a project idea

Steps:
1. Use the project list to select your project.
2. Look up the directions on the "BT" page given.
3. Mark an X in the project box after you complete your project.
2. Write the title of the book and the completion date as shown on page 111.
3. Place a star by a project you especially liked.

Reading Project List Example

BT Page	Reading Project	Helen Keller 1-8-93	Castle in Attic 2-25-93									
42	Author Profile											
129	Advertise-a-Book Poster		X									
112	Bookmark											
74	Book-Sell											
76	Book-Talk	X										
88	Bubble Gum Review											
122	Character Mask											
116	Character Report Card											
44	Illustrator Profile											
40	Letter to an Author											
86	Pizza Report											
114	Puppet Character											
82	Remarkable Review											
126	Setting Map											
118	Story Cube											
57	Story Map (Individual)											
58	Story Map (Group)											
120	Story Quilt											
69	Venn Diagram											
124	Wanted Poster											

Making a Bookmark

This project is great for new readers. It makes reading their special book even more fun. After the bookmark is finished you can make it more durable by covering it with clear contact paper or laminating it.

Materials:

Form (copy – page 156)	Scissors
Popsicle sticks/ribbon	Glue
Crayons/marker/pencil	Tagboard/Paper

Goal:

To create a special bookmark for the book you are reading

Steps:

1. Decide on the design of your bookmark. Some examples are on page 113.
2. Draw the shape onto tagboard/cardboard.
3. Cut out the shape and draw your design.
4. Glue a popsicle stick, ribbon or strip of paper to the back if you want to make it longer.

Just for Fun:

Make a bookmark as a gift for someone who might like the book

Bookmark Examples

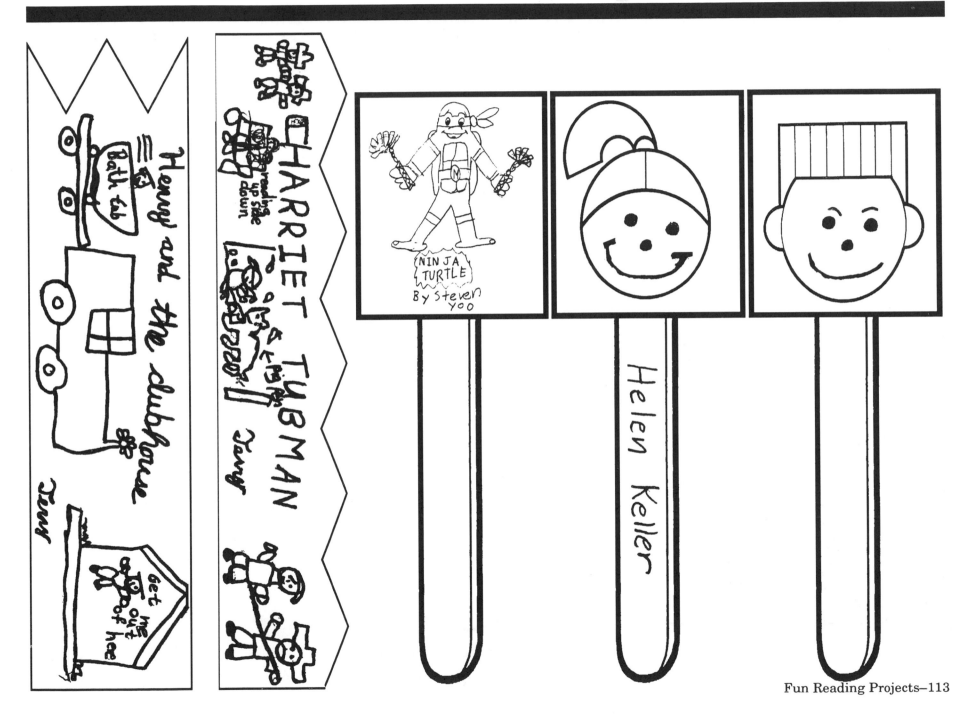

Making Puppet Characters

This project was recommended by Suzie Fiebig's 2nd-grade class at Juanita Elementary in Kirkland, WA. Their puppet characters were created around scenes from "Frog and Toad are Friends," by Arnold Lobel. They used their puppets in a group dramatization of a specific scene. It was great fun.

Materials:

Paper sack/paper plate	Scissors
Popsicle sticks	Glue
Construction paper	Markers/crayons

Goal:

To retell a scene from your book using the puppet characters you make

Steps:

1. Read your book and decide which part (scene) you want to retell.
2. Choose the characters for your retell.
3. Choose the type of puppet you want to make, and using the directions on page 115, make your puppet character(s).

Just for Fun:

Draw setting on paper and use it for scenery
Make a puppet character out of an old sock

Puppet Character Directions

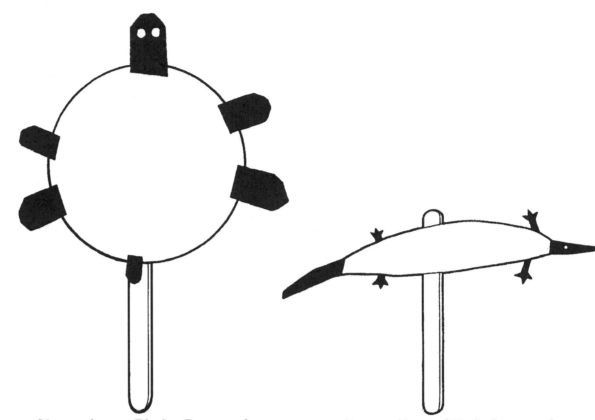

Steps for a Sack Puppet

1. Find a small paper sack.
2. Draw the character's arms, legs, head, and top and bottom lips on paper. Color them.
3. Cut out each of your drawings.
4. Glue them onto the bag as shown above.
5. Put your hand inside the bag and move your character's lips as you talk for it.

Steps for a Plate Puppet

1. Find a popsicle stick and paper plate.
2. Draw the character's arms, legs, head (tail if it needs one) onto construction paper. Color them.
3. Cut out each of your drawings.
4. Glue them onto the outside of a paper plate as shown above.
5. Glue a popsicle stick to the inside of the plate.

Steps for a Stick Puppet

1. Find a popsicle stick.
2. Draw the character's body on construction paper. Color.
3. Cut out your drawing.
4. Glue it to the popsicle stick.

Making a Character Report Card

Lori Blevins Gonwick's 3rd-grade students at Juanita Elementary in Kirkland, WA, thoroughly enjoy grading a character in a story and heartily recommend it.

Materials:
Form (copy – page 157)
Pencil/markers

Goal:
To write a report card for a character in the book you are reading

Steps:
1. Read your book.
2. Choose the character for the report card.
3. Grade the character on his/her behavior in the story.
4. Write in comments to describe why the character earned this grade.

Just for Fun:
Create your own report card for a character

Character Report Card Example

Character

Character Report Card

E	Outstanding
S+	Good
S	Satisfactory
S-	Needs improving
N	Needs to try again

Student: Kimi
Teacher: Steven Yoo
Grade: 4th grade

"It's the Soup that Made Me Sad"

Book Title

BEHAVIOR	GRADE	COMMENTS
Positive attitude:	S-	Because she didn't clean up her room up.
Follows directions:	S-	
Helpful:	S	
Demonstrates thoughtfulness of others:	S+	She was nice to a man in a restrong.
Pays attention:	N	She couldn't find her baseball mitt.
Assumes and carries through responsibilities:	S+	She improved when she cleaned up her room.
Other comments:		

Making a Story Cube

The story cube was recommended by Lori Blevins Gonwick's 3rd-grade classroom as one of their favorites. There are many ways to share a story cube. The focus can be on story characters, plot, story scenes etc. Small boxes can also be purchased at art supply stores.

Materials:

Tagboard   Markers/pencil/crayons
Scissors   Glue

Steps:

1. Determine the size of your story cube and trace six square panels onto tagboard in the shape shown on the next page. Cut your cube out.
2. Select the story you want to retell with your box. Decide what you want to draw and/or write on the outside of your cube. Draw and write on each square. Note: panel 1,2, and 6 are drawn straight. Panel 3,4, and 5 are drawn facing out (see example on the next page).
3. Fold the cube panels as shown and glue them together.
4. Share your special story cube with friends.

Story Cube Directions

Step 1

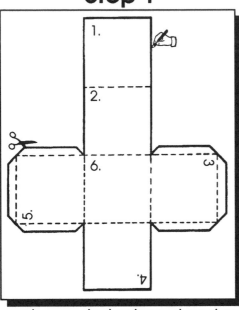

Trace your box onto tagboard and cut it out.

Step 2

Draw and write the things you want to share from the story in each square. Note the direction each square's drawing is facing.

Step 3

Turn the illustrated side over and fold it into a box shape (as shown above). Glue each square edge to another.

Step 4

Erin's Book Box for *One Hundred Dresses* by Eleanor Estes

After the glue dries you can share your story cube with your friends.

Making a Story Quilt

The Story Quilt was recommended by Valerie Marshall and Martha Ivy's 4th-grade classroom at Crista McAuliffe Elementary in Redmond, WA. As one of the teachers reads a story to the class, students take turns illustrating a scene. By the end of the book, they have created a class story quilt.

Materials:
Pencil/markers   Glue

Construction paper/paper   Scissors

Goal:
To share a book through a drawn quilt made up of scenes from a favorite story

Steps:
1. Read your book.
2. Re-read your favorite scenes.
3. Decide how many pieces you will include in your story quilt.
4. List the scenes you want to include.
5. Draw each scene onto the same size paper.
6. Use a construction paper border around the outside of the quilt and between the quilt pieces.
7. Re-tell the story using the pictures from your story quilt.

Story Quilt Example

The Master Puppeteer by Katherine Paterson

Story Quilt by Juleah Swanson

Making a Character Mask

Valerie Marshall and Martha Ivy's 4th-graders filled their room with character masks hanging in a row. They took turns guessing who each character mask represented. They used different colored and textured pantyhose to get just the right look for their masks. This is a great recycling project.

Materials:
Pantyhose leg (used)   Yarn/ribbon
Hanger (wire)   Construction paper
Markers/crayons   Glue

Goal:
To create a mask of a character in the book
  you are reading

Steps:
1. Stretch out the bottom of the wire hanger.
2. Slip the pantyhose around the hanger and tie it at the top with yarn.
3. Cut yarn or ribbon for hair and glue it to the mask.
4. Draw and cut paper eyes, nose and mouth.
5. Paste face onto the mask and hang up for everyone to guess the character.

Character Mask Directions

Step 1

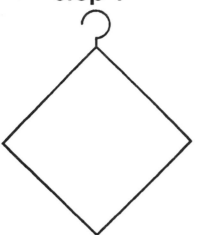

Stretch out a hanger by pulling down on the bottom.

Step 2

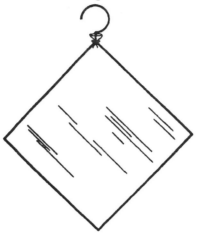

Slip pantyhose leg around hanger and tie at the top.

Step 3

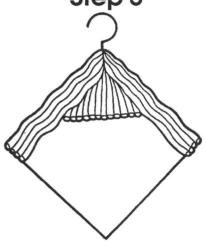

Cut yarn or ribbon for hair and glue to the mask.

Step 4

Draw eyes, nose, and mouth onto contruction paper. Cut them out.

Step 5

Glue the face pieces onto your character mask.

Character Masks

Hang your mask up with others and guess who the characters are.

Making a Character Wanted Poster

Japhy Whalen's 4th- and 5th-grade students at Graham Hill Elementary in Seattle, WA, recommended the Character Wanted Poster as their favorite reading project. It's fun to create your own design and layout.

Materials:
Paper
Marker/pencil
Book

Goal:
To create a wanted poster of your character to share with your friends

Steps:
1. Decide upon the character for your wanted poster.
2. Think about how you want your poster to look and what you want to say on it.
3. Using the information you've learned about the character in the story, draw his/her picture in the center of the page.
4. Write in the information you've chosen to include and draw an outside border.

Wanted Poster Example

WANTED

NAME: Moon Shadow
Height: "6 5"
Weight: 160 LB.
Hair Color: Jet Black
Eye Color: Dark Blue
Scars: None
Other: Fast runner
hard to catch.

Wanted: Suspected of stealing
clothes from drycleaning customers.
Reward: $10,000.00
Contact Person: Brandon Schnierer
Telephone: 1-800 Wanted
Where To: Alcatraz Prison

WANTED

Making a Setting Map

Joyce Standing's 5th-grade class at the Overlake School in Redmond, WA, recommends the Setting Map as a great reading project. It's fun, it's messy, and kids thoroughly enjoy creating a lasting work of art. This is another project that recycles household items.

Materials:

Old newspapers   Tempera paint
Wallpaper paste   Recycled objects
Paint brush   Corrugated cardboard

Steps:

1. Decide what setting you want your map to represent and design the map layout. Cut cardboard for the map base.
2. Find used items to create houses, buildings, etc. (milk cartons, boxes, cans).
3. Tear newspaper into long thin strips. Pour wallpaper paste into a bowl and pull strips through it as you squeeze extra paste off.
4. Laying strips in the same direction, cover the base and positioned map objects. Repeat this process across the last strips four more times.
5. When dry (1-2 days), paint objects and base.

Setting Map Directions

Step 1

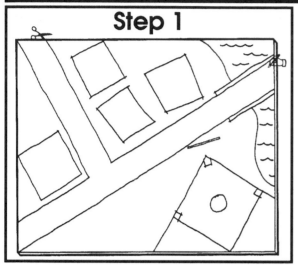

Design the layout of your setting map. Cut cardboard to create the base of your map.

Step 2

Collect used items for your setting. Small milk cartons, boxes, cans and other household items work well.

Step 3

Tear newspaper into long thin strips. Pour wallpaper paste in a bowl and pull strips through. Squeeze them.

Step 4

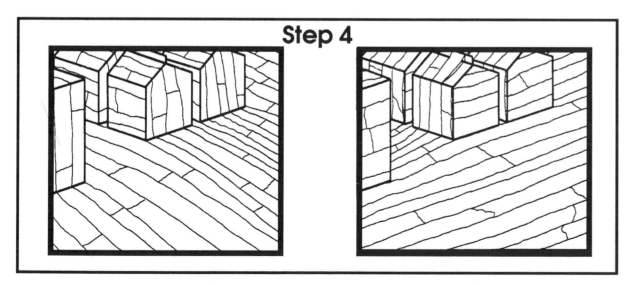

Laying strips in the same direction, cover the base and objects.

Apply four more layers of strips across the earlier strips. Let them dry.

Step 5

Paint the base and the objects on your map. Share it with others.

Making an Advertise–a–Book Poster

An Advertise-a-Book Poster was recommended by students in many different classrooms. Its creative possibilities are limitless. This is a good project for many different grade levels.

Materials:
Tagboard/poster board
Markers/pencil

Goal:
To create a poster that will make people want to read your book

Steps:
1. Decide which book you want to advertise.
2. Think about the most interesting parts of the story.
3. Lay out your ideas on a piece of paper.
4. Later, come back to your poster design ideas and change anything that doesn't fit.
5. Draw your poster onto tagboard.

Just for Fun:
Make a collage out of magazine photographs

Advertise–a–Book Poster Example

Shrink into "The Castle in the Attic" for...

Adventure

Excitement

Suspense

Book by Elizabeth Winthrop
Poster by Nick

Project Supply Sheet Example

My Project Supply Sheet

Name: *Nick*

My Project is: _Advertise-a-book Poster_

To do my project I will need:

Writing Tools
- ✔ pencil(s)
- ✔ marker(s)
- ___ pen(s)
- ✔ crayons
- ___

Art Supplies
- ___ glue
- ___ paste
- ___ wallpaper paste
- ✔ scissors
- ___ paint
- ___ paint brush
- ___ glitter
- ___ stickers
- ___ tape
- ___

Paper Supplies
- ___ form (page #   )
- ___ plain paper
- ___ lined paper
- ___ construction paper
- ✔ tagboard
- ___ butcher paper
- ___ newspaper
- ___ cardboard
- ___ corrugated cardboard
- ___ contact paper
- ___

Other Possible Items
- ✔ book
- ___ popsicle stick
- ___ paper sack
- ___ ribbon
- ___ yarn
- ___ envelope
- ___ stamp
- ___ video camera
- ___ pantyhose
- ___ hanger
- ___ recycled objects
- ___

Chapter 7
Reference Books

Reference Books

Author	Book Title	Publisher
Brown, Hazel Cambourne, Brian	*Read and Retell*	Heinemann Educational Books, 1990
Calkins, Lucy McCormick	*Lessons from a Child*	Heinemann Educational Books, 1983
Hornsby, David Sukarna, Deborah Parry, Jo-Ann	*Read On: A Conference Approach to Reading*	Heinemann Educational Books, 1986
Peterson, Ralph Eeds, Maryann	*Grand Conversations: Literature Groups in Action*	Scholastic, 1990
Routman, Reggie	*Invitations*	Heinemann Educational Books, 1991
Short, Kathy Pierce, Katherine	*Talking About Books*	Heinemann Educational Books, 1990
Weaver, Constance	*Reading Process and Practice: From Socio-Psycholinguistics to Whole Language*	Heinemann Educational Books, 1988
Wilde, Sandra	*You Kan Red This!: Spelling and Punctuation for Whole Language Classrooms K-6*	Heinemann Educational Books, 1992

Chapter 8

Forms to Copy

Interest Sheet

1. Things I like to do at home

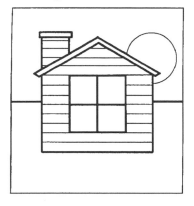

2. Things I like to do at school

3. My favorite movies and t.v. shows

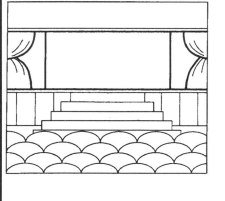 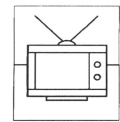

4. Things I wonder about

Name:

<u>Book Ideas</u>

1. _____

_____

_____

2. _____

_____

_____

3. _____

_____

4. _____

_____

_____

Forms from <u>Book-Talk: Exciting Literature Experiences for Kids</u>, a MicNik Publication

Name:

Books I Really Want To Read !

Title	Author	Genre	I read it! ✔

Name:

My Reading Record

Date	My Book Title	Page

 Forms from <u>Book-Talk: Exciting Literature Experiences for Kids</u>, a MicNik Publication

Genre Toppings

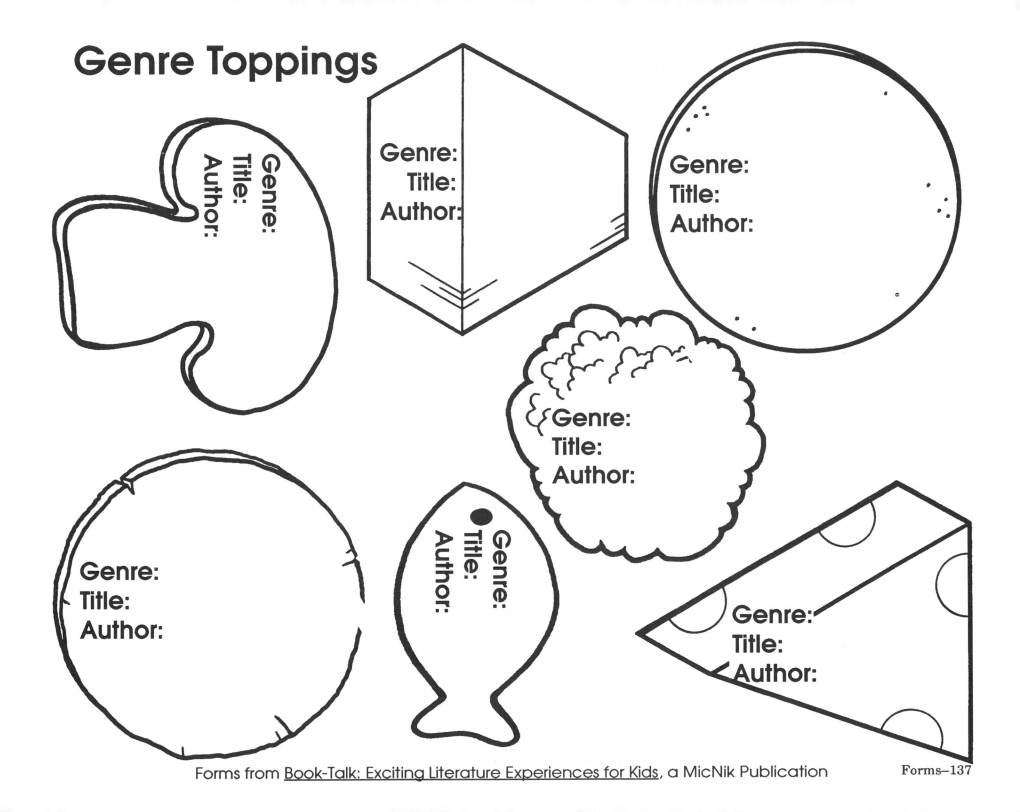

Genre:
Title:
Author:

Genre:
Title:
Author:

Genre:
Title:
Author:

Genre:
Title:
Author:

Genre:
Title:
Author:

Genre:
Title:
Author:

Genre:
Title:
Author:

Forms from <u>Book-Talk: Exciting Literature Experiences for Kids</u>, a MicNik Publication

My Favorite Authors

My Name:

Author's name

Author's name

Author's name

Author's name

Author's name

Forms from <u>Book-Talk: Exciting Literature Experiences for Kids</u>, a MicNik Publication

Author Profile

Name:
Date:

**Author's name, age
and home**

Author's family

**Number of books written and
some book titles**

Favorite type of writing

Why author likes to write

Forms from Book-Talk: Exciting Literature Experiences for Kids, a MicNik Publication

Illustrator Profile

Name:

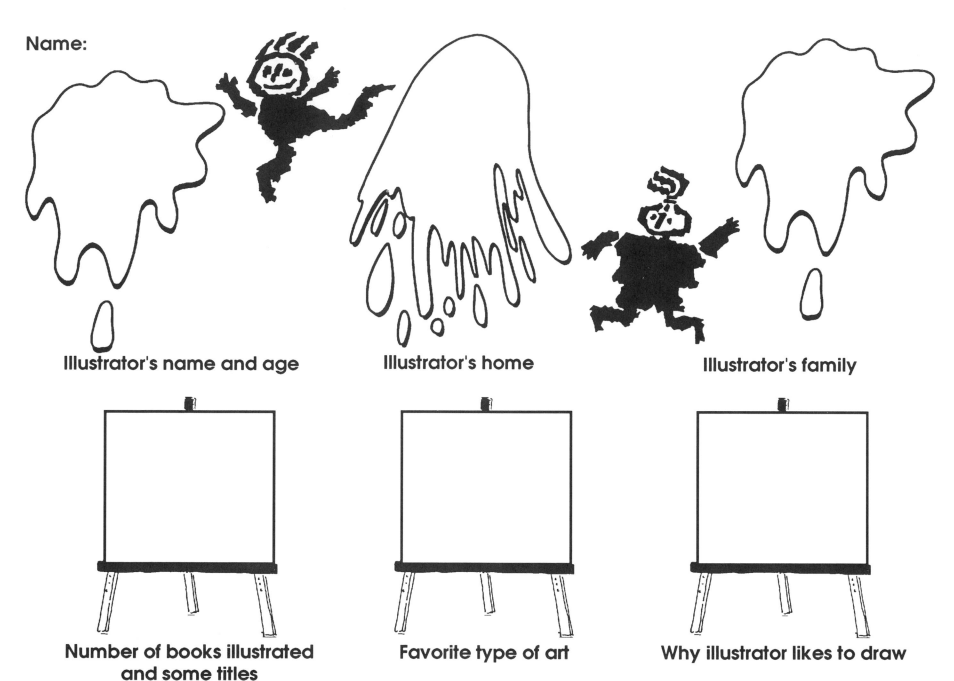

Illustrator's name and age

Illustrator's home

Illustrator's family

Number of books illustrated and some titles

Favorite type of art

Why illustrator likes to draw

Forms from <u>Book-Talk: Exciting Literature Experiences for Kids</u>, a MicNik Publication

My Favorite Illustrators

Name:

Story Sheet

Things I noticed in the story

Beginning

(The Foot Book by Dr. Seuss)

Middle

End

Feelings I had

(Circle the feelings)

How this story reminds me of my life

Forms from Book-Talk: Exciting Literature Experiences for Kids, a MicNik Publication

Story Map

Name:
Title:
Author:

CHARACTERS ▲   **SETTING ▼**

PROBLEM(S)▼

SOLUTION(S)▼

CONCLUSION ▲

Forms from <u>Book-Talk: Exciting Literature Experiences for Kids</u>, a MicNik Publication

Venn Diagram

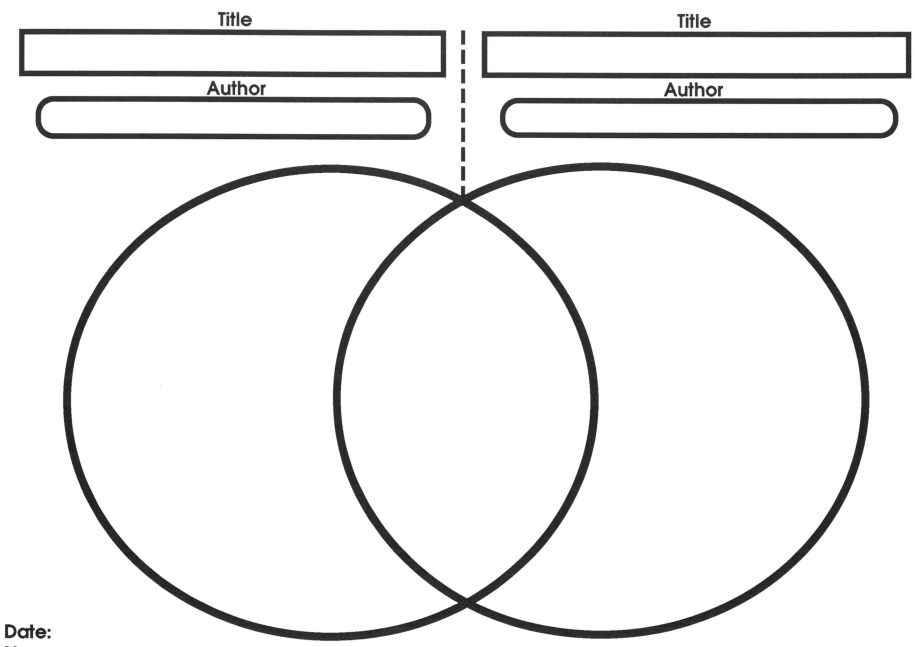

Title

Author

Title

Author

Forms from <u>Book-Talk: Exciting Literature Experiences for Kids</u>, a MicNik Publication

Character Comparison Sheet

Character 1:

Character 2:

CHARACTER SIMILARITIES

CHARACTER DIFFERENCES

Remarkable Reviewer

This Book's HOT!

My Challenge Scale
Low 1 • 2 • 3 • 4 • 5 High

Name:

Title

Author

Illustrator

Characters

Summary of Story

Setting

I chose this book because: _____
_____
_____

My favorite part of this book was: _____
_____
_____

Forms from <u>Book-Talk: Exciting Literature Experiences for Kids</u>, a MicNik Publication

Remarkable Reviewer
This Book's NOT HOT!

My Challenge Scale
Low 1•2•3•4•5 High

Name:

Title

Author

Illustrator

Short Summary

I chose this book because: _____

_____

_____

I didn't like this book because: _____

_____

_____

_____

Remarkable Reviewer

This Book is just <u>OK</u>

My Challenge Scale
Low 1•2•3•4•5 High

Name:

Title

Author	**Illustrator**

Characters	**Setting**

Plot Summary

I chose this book because: _____

_____

I think this book is just OK because: _____

_____

I would recommend it to a friend: ☐ YES ☐ NO
Please explain:_____

_____

Forms from <u>Book-Talk: Exciting Literature Experiences for Kids</u>, a MicNik Publication

Pizza Reports

Canadian Bacon Report

_____
Title of the book

Author_____
Illustrator_____

# of pages____

        easy❑ medium❑ challenge❑

Where does the story take place?

_____

_____

_____

Do you recommend this book? Y N

**Draw a picture of
the setting on the back**

Sausage Report

Title _____
Author_____
Illustrator_____
# of pages____ easy❑ medium❑ challenge❑

What happens at the beginning of the story?

_____

_____

What happens in the middle of the story?

_____

_____

What happens at the end of the story?

_____

_____

Do you like the ending?
Yes ❑ No ❑

Pizza Reports

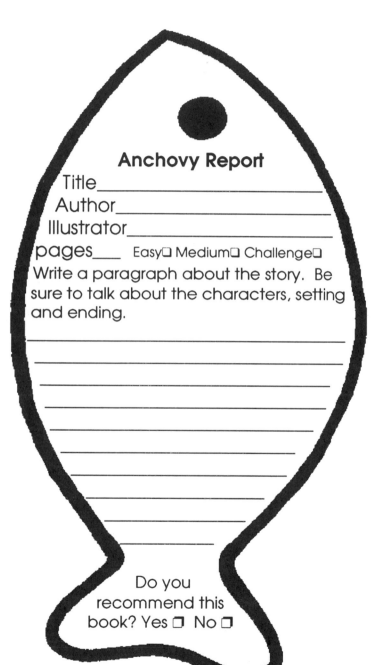

Anchovy Report

Title_____

Author_____

Illustrator_____

pages____ Easy☐ Medium☐ Challenge☐

Write a paragraph about the story. Be sure to talk about the characters, setting and ending.

_____

_____

_____

_____

_____

_____

_____

_____

Do you recommend this book? Yes ☐ No ☐

Pepperoni Report

Title_____

Author_____

Illustrator_____

# of pages____   easy ☐ medium☐ challenge☐

What is the "Main Character's" goal?

_____

Do you like the "Main Character"? Why?

_____

_____

If you were the "Main Character" what other ways would you try to reach the goal?

_____

_____

_____

_____

_____

• Re-write the ending on the back

Forms from <u>Book-Talk: Exciting Literature Experiences for Kids</u>, a MicNik Publication

Bubble Gum Review

Name:

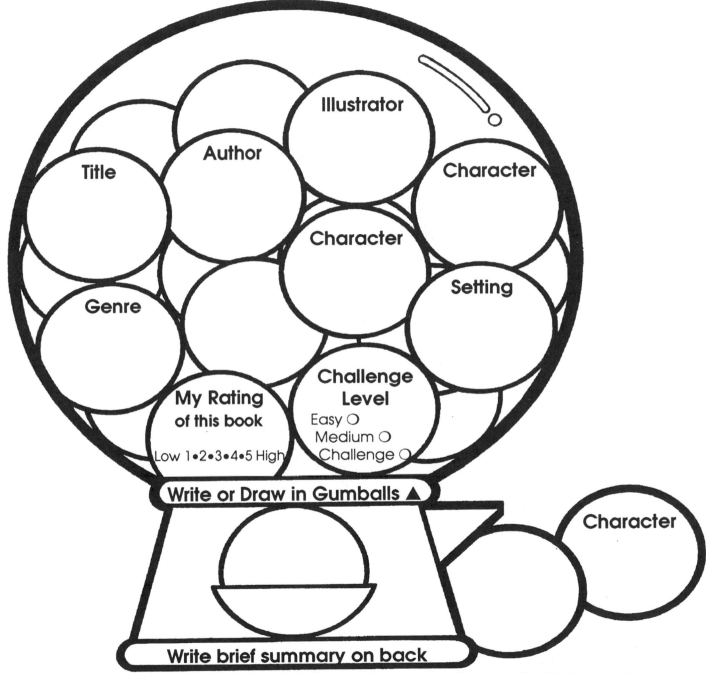

Illustrator

Author

Title

Character

Character

Genre

Setting

My Rating
of this book

Low 1•2•3•4•5 High

Challenge
Level

Easy ○
Medium ○
Challenge ○

Write or Draw in Gumballs ▲

Character

Write brief summary on back

Forms from <u>Book-Talk: Exciting Literature Experiences for Kids</u>, a MicNik Publication

Book Ballot and Book-Talk Notes

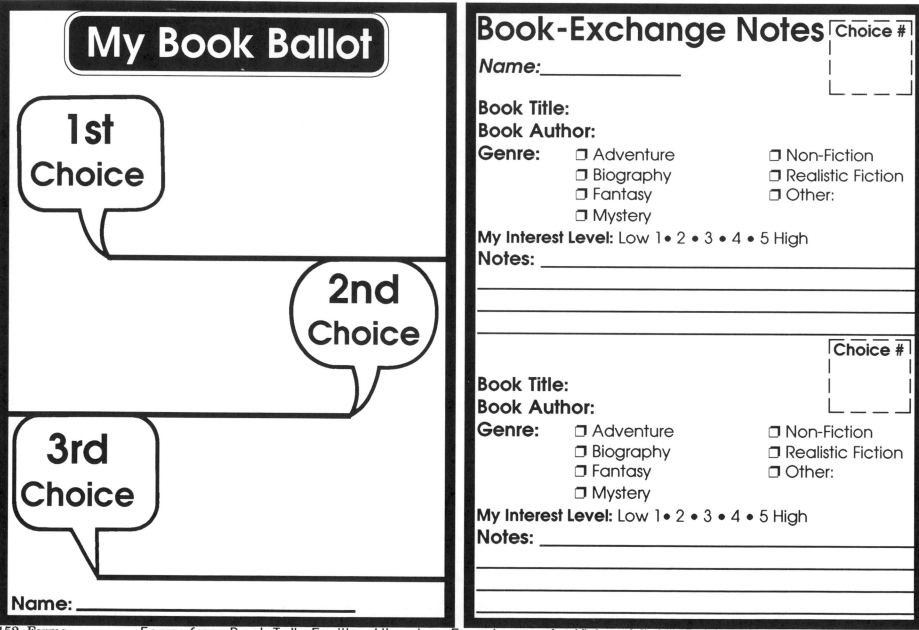

My Book Ballot

1st Choice

2nd Choice

3rd Choice

Name: _____

Book-Exchange Notes Choice #

Name: _____

Book Title:
Book Author:
Genre:
- ❐ Adventure
- ❐ Biography
- ❐ Fantasy
- ❐ Mystery
- ❐ Non-Fiction
- ❐ Realistic Fiction
- ❐ Other:

My Interest Level: Low 1 • 2 • 3 • 4 • 5 High
Notes: _____
_____
_____
_____

Choice #

Book Title:
Book Author:
Genre:
- ❐ Adventure
- ❐ Biography
- ❐ Fantasy
- ❐ Mystery
- ❐ Non-Fiction
- ❐ Realistic Fiction
- ❐ Other:

My Interest Level: Low 1 • 2 • 3 • 4 • 5 High
Notes: _____
_____
_____

Forms from <u>Book-Talk: Exciting Literature Experiences for Kids</u>, a MicNik Publication

Literature Group Self-Evaluation

Date	Our group goal for today was:	Met goal Yes No	In my literature group today I learned...	+ ✓ − I give myself a

Literature Group Record Keeping

Student's Name	Preparation			Participation: low 1•2•3 high			
	Brought Book	Read Book	Noted his/her Interests	In group	Response Quality	Text Reference	Listening Skills
				☐	☐	☐	☐
				☐	☐	☐	☐
				☐	☐	☐	☐
				☐	☐	☐	☐
				☐	☐	☐	☐
				☐	☐	☐	☐
				☐	☐	☐	☐

Notes:

Forms from <u>Book-Talk: Exciting Literature Experiences for Kids</u>, a MicNik Publication

Reading Project List

BT Page	Reading Project											
42	Author Profile											
129	Advertise-a-Book Poster											
112	Bookmark											
74	Book-Sell											
76	Book-Talk											
88	Bubble Gum Review											
122	Character Mask											
116	Character Report Card											
44	Illustrator Profile											
40	Letter to an Author											
86	Pizza Report											
114	Puppet Character											
82	Remarkable Review											
126	Setting Map											
118	Story Cube											
57	Story Map (Individual)											
58	Story Map (Group)											
120	Story Quilt											
69	Venn Diagram											
124	Wanted Poster											

Bookmark Templates

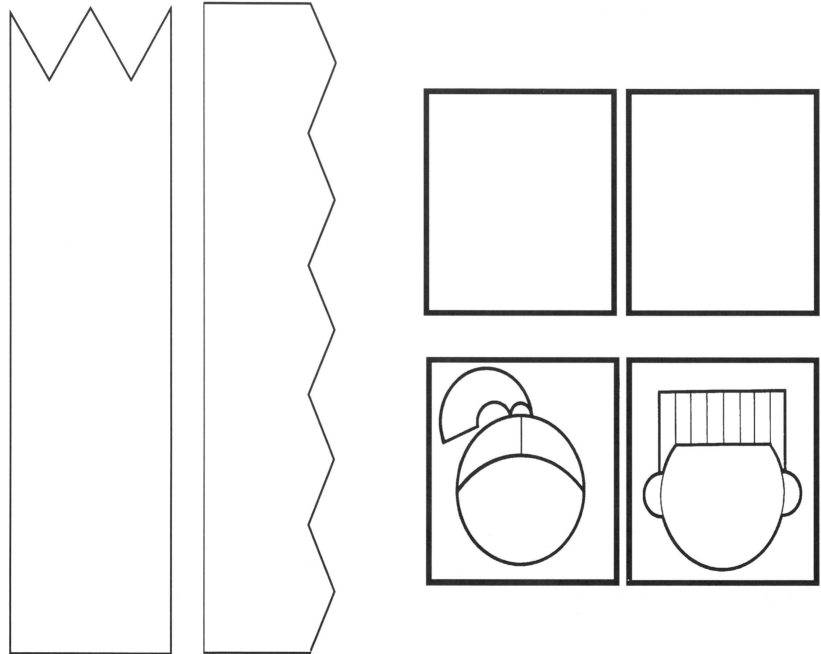

Forms from <u>Book-Talk: Exciting Literature Experiences for Kids</u>, a MicNik Publication

Character
Report Card

Character	E Outstanding S+ Good S Satisfactory S- Needs improving N Needs to try again

Student: _____

Teacher: _____

Grade: _____

Book Title

BEHAVIOR	GRADE	COMMENTS
Positive attitude:		
Follows directions:		
Helpful:		
Demonstrates thoughtfulness of others:		
Pays attention:		
Assumes and carries through responsibilities:		
Other comments:		

My Project Supply Sheet

Name:

My Project is: _____

To do my project I will need:

Writing Tools

___ pencil(s)
___ marker(s)
___ pen(s)
___ crayons
___
___
___

Art Supplies

___ glue
___ paste
___ wallpaper paste
___ scissors
___ paint
___ paint brush
___ glitter
___ stickers
___ tape
___
___

Paper Supplies

___ form page #
___ plain paper
___ lined paper
___ construction paper
___ tagboard
___ butcher paper
___ newspaper
___ cardboard
___ corrugated cardboard
___ contact paper
___
___
___

Other Possible Items

___ book
___ popsicle stick
___ paper sack
___ ribbon
___ yarn
___ envelope
___ stamp
___ video camera
___ pantyhose
___ hanger
___ recycled objects
___
___

Forms from <u>Book-Talk: Exciting Literature Experiences for Kids</u>, a MicNik Publication

ABOUT THE AUTHOR

Michelle received her undergraduate and graduate degrees at the University of Washington. She is an educational consultant and author. Michelle is 38 years old and lives in the Pacific Northwest with her son and husband. She loves writing and working with young authors and readers.

Her first book, *Through My Eyes*, was co-authored with her son, Nicholas, when he was five years old and illustrated by the children in his kindergarten class. Her second book, *Book-Write*, guides young authors through the five step writing process, enabling them to write their own books. Michelle always includes children in the creation of her books.

MicNik Publications

michelle o'brien-palmer

BOOK-TALK
exciting literature experiences for kids

illustrations by denny driver

Book-Talk does for reading what Book-Write does for writing. It is a fun, clear, easy-to-follow resource guide for teachers and parents who want to encourage a lifelong love of literature. Book-Talk is filled with examples from real kids and classrooms.

11" x 8 1/2" • 160 pages • $16.95
ISBN 1-879235-02-1
(WA State tax – $1.45)

michelle o'brien-palmer

BOOK-WRITE
a creative bookmaking guide for young authors

illustrations by shannon rubin

A fun, easy-to-follow, bookmaking guide for young authors. Filled with examples of other young authors' books. A wonderful resource for teachers and parents interested in the writing process. Reproducible forms for use in the classroom or at home.

11" x 8 1/2" • 128 pages • $16.95
ISBN 1-879235-01-3
(WA State tax – $1.45)

THROUGH MY EYES

O'Brien-Palmer and Palmer

A look at life through the eyes of a young child. Co-authored and illustrated by children – the poetry in "Through My Eyes" has brought joy to readers all over the country. There is space for young authors to write their own poems in the back of this book.

5 1/2" x 8 1/2" • 33 pages • $6.95
ISBN 1-879235-00-5
(WA State tax – $.60)

ORDER FORM

15% discount on orders
of 5 or more books

MicNik Publications

P.O. Box 3041 • Kirkland, WA 98083
(206) 881-6476

QUANTITY	TITLE OF BOOK	PRICE
	Book-Talk: Exciting Literature Experiences for Kids	
	Book-Write: A Creative Bookmaking Guide for Young Authors	
	Through My Eyes	

Send to:

SHIPPING CHART	
USPS	
$2.90 - *Book-Write/Book-Talk*	
$ .50 - each additional "	
$1.00 - *Through My Eyes*	
$ .50 - each additional "	

Book Total	
If 5 books -15% off	
Sales tax -WA only	
Postage/handling	
Total Enclosed	

Please make checks payable to MicNik Publications